Street by Street

HERTFORD
WELWYN GARDEN CITY
HATFIELD, WARE, WELWYN
Brookmans Park, Codicote, Essendon, Oaklands, St Margarets, Stanstead Abbotts, Tewin, Wadesmill, Welham Green

C000216683

1st edition September 2002

© Automobile Association Developments Limited 2002

Ordnance Survey® This product includes map data licensed from Ordnance Survey® with the permission of the Controller of Her Majesty's Stationery Office. © Crown copyright 2002. All rights reserved. Licence No: 399221.

Published by AA Publishing (a trading name of Automobile Association Developments Limited, whose registered office is Millstream, Maidenhead Road, Windsor, Berkshire SL4 5GD. Registered number 1878835).

The Post Office is a registered trademark of Post Office Ltd. in the UK and other countries.

Schools address data provided by Education Direct.

One-way street data provided by:

Tele Atlas © Tele Atlas N.V.

Mapping produced by the Cartographic Department of The Automobile Association. A01100

A CIP Catalogue record for this book is available from the British Library.

Printed by GRAFIASA S.A., Porto, Portugal

Ref: ML189

Key to map pages	ii-iii
Key to map symbols	iv-1
Street by Street	2-43
Index – towns & villages	44
Index – streets	45-50
Index – featured places	50-51

ii

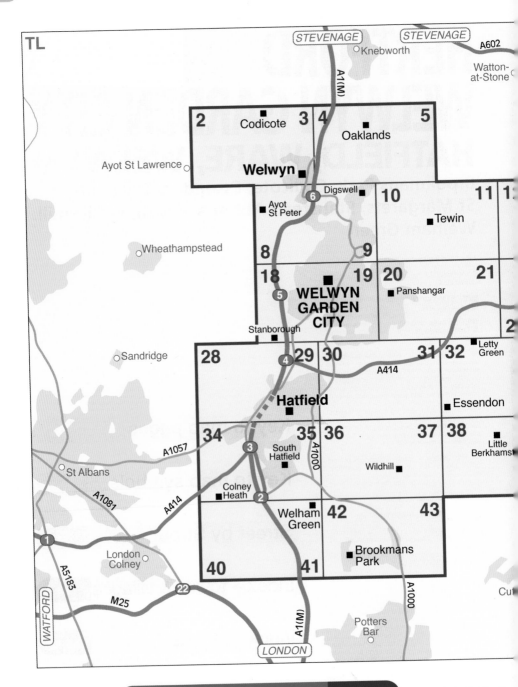

TL

STEVENAGE STEVENAGE A602
Knebworth
Watton-at-Stone

A1(M)

2 Codicote **3** **4** Oaklands **5**

Ayot St Lawrence

Welwyn

6 Digswell

Ayot St Peter **10** **11** 1
Tewin

Wheathampstead

8 **9**

18 **19** **20** **21**
5 **WELWYN** Panshangar
GARDEN
CITY
Stanborough 2

28 **29** **30** **31** **32** Letty Green
4 A414
Sandridge
Hatfield Essendon

34 **35** **36** **37** **38**
A1057 3 South Little
Hatfield Berkhams
St Albans A1000 Wildhill
A1081 Colney
A414 Heath 2 **42** **43**
Welham
London Green
Colney **40** **41** Brookmans
Park
1

WATFORD A5183 M25 22 A1(M) A1000 Cut

Potters Bar

LONDON

Scale of map pages   1:15,000   4.2 inches to 1 mile

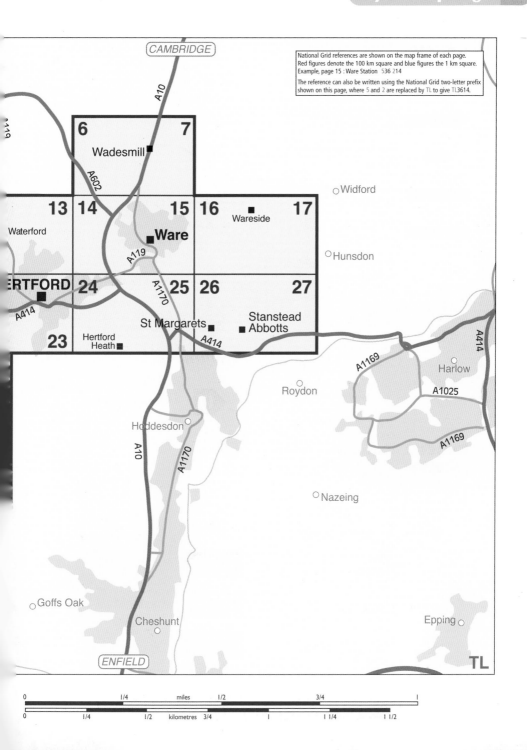

CAMBRIDGE

National Grid references are shown on the map frame of each page.
Red figures denote the 100 km square and blue figures the 1 km square.
Example, page 15 : Ware Station 536 214

The reference can also be written using the National Grid two-letter prefix
shown on this page, where 5 and 2 are replaced by TL to give TL3614.

A10

A119

A602

6   **7**

Wadesmill ■

13 **14**   **15** **16**   **17**

Waterford

Wareside ■

○ Widford

■ **Ware**

A119

○ Hunsdon

ERTFORD **24**   **25** **26**   **27**

A1170

A414

St Margarets ■

Stanstead
Abbotts ■

23

Hertford
Heath ■

A414

A1169

Harlow ○

A1025

A1169

A414

○ Roydon

Hoddesdon ○

A10

A1170

○ Nazeing

○ Goffs Oak

Cheshunt ○

Epping ○

ENFIELD

TL

| 0 | 1/4 | miles | 1/2 | 3/4 | 1 |

| 0 | 1/4 | 1/2 | kilometres | 3/4 | 1 | 1 1/4 | 1 1/2 |

Symbol	Description
Junction 9	Motorway & junction
Services	Motorway service area
	Primary road single/dual carriageway
Services	Primary road service area
	A road single/dual carriageway
	B road single/dual carriageway
	Other road single/dual carriageway
	Minor/private road, access may be restricted
← ←	One-way street
	Pedestrian area
	Track or footpath
	Road under construction
	Road tunnel
AA	AA Service Centre
P	Parking
P+	Park & Ride
	Bus/coach station
	Railway & main railway station
	Railway & minor railway station
	Underground station
	Light railway & station
++++++++++	Preserved private railway
LC	Level crossing
•—•—•—•—•	Tramway
- - - - - -	Ferry route
....	Airport runway
— · — · — · —	County, administrative boundary
vvvvvvvvvv	Mounds
17	Page continuation
	River/canal, lake, pier
	Aqueduct, lock, weir
465 ▲ Winter Hill	Peak (with height in metres)
	Beach
	Woodland
	Park
	Cemetery
	Built-up area

Symbol	Description		Symbol	Description
	Featured building			Abbey, cathedral or priory
	City wall			Castle
A&E	Hospital with 24-hour A&E department			Historic house or building
PO	Post Office		Wakehurst Place NT	National Trust property
	Public library			Museum or art gallery
i	Tourist Information Centre			Roman antiquity
	Petrol station Major suppliers only			Ancient site, battlefield or monument
†	Church/chapel			Industrial interest
	Public toilets			Garden
	Toilet with disabled facilities			Arboretum
PH	Public house AA recommended			Farm or animal centre
	Restaurant AA inspected			Zoological or wildlife collection
	Theatre or performing arts centre			Bird collection
	Cinema			Nature reserve
	Golf course		V	Visitor or heritage centre
▲	Camping AA inspected			Country park
	Caravan Site AA inspected			Cave
	Camping & caravan site AA inspected			Windmill
	Theme park			Distillery, brewery or vineyard

2

River Mimram

A
B
Codicote Heath
C
D

To

5 20
21

Kimpton Mill

1

Kimpton Road

18

Codicote Lodge

▷ Heath Hill
Heath Hill Road Lane

Meadow Way

C
J
S

Tanyard Lane

Kimpton Road

2

Codicote Bottom

Dark Lane

Abbotshay

Kimpton Road

River Mimram

3

17

Lord Mead Lane

St Albans

+

PH

4

's Corner ardian Hall NT)

Ayot St Lawrence

Kimpton Road

5

Bride Hall Lane

216

Codicote Road

Ryefield Farm

Hill Farm

Hill

Farm

5 20

21

A
B
C
D

I grid square represents 500 metres

Woolmer
Green

Green

Brookbridge Lane

Mardle Fry

E

F

G

H

Hawkins Hall
Farm

Watton Road

Gover's
Green

Datchworth
Green

Bramfield Road

I

2

Coltsfoot Lane

Welches Farm

Bull's
Green

3

White Horse Lane

Burnham
Green

Bishops Road

Purcello
Close

Queen

Hoo Lane

4

Harmer Green Lane

Two Oaks Dr

Tylers Wood

Burnham Close

Burnham

Green

Orchard

Cowpers Way

Firs

Walk

5

Tewin Close

Tewin
Wood

Desborough Drive

East Riding

West Riding

Badgers Walk

Road

E

F

G

H

10

Tewin Hill
Farm

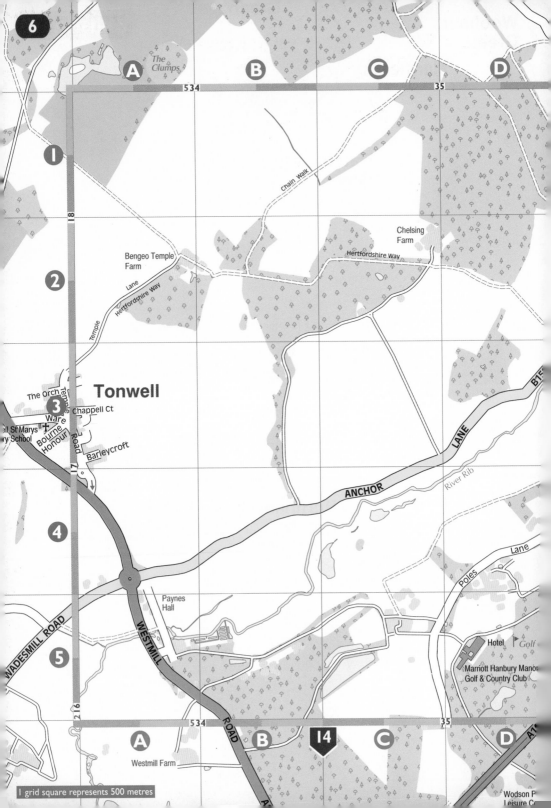

Puller Memorial CE Primary School

Marshall's Lane

E   **F**   Marshall's   **G**   High Cross   **H**

36   37

Poplar Close

Works

North Drive

A10(T)

I

18

Youngsbury

2

Harcamlow Way

Vadesmill

Millfield

Hertfordshire Way

Dellfield   Works   Youngsbury Lane

Thundridge CE Primary School   PO   Ermine Street

Old Church Lane

Old Church Lane

3

Hertfordshire Way

17

Thundridge   Ducketts Wood

Woodlands Road

Cold Christmas Lane

Cold Christmas Lane

Cold Christmas

A10(T)

PH

SG12

4

Thundridge Business Park

Cowards

Ashridge Common

216

5

Harcamlow Way

36   37

E   **F**   **15**   **G**   **H**

Wodson Park Track

Round House

Fanhams

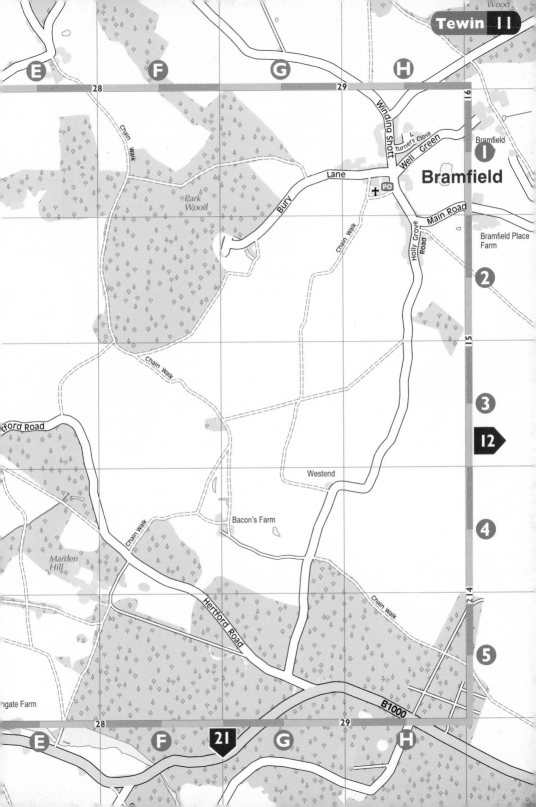

Moles Farm

E F **7** G H

36 37

Wodson Park Track

Round House

Fanhams Hall

I

Salmons Close
Heath
Chiltern Close
Rockfield
St Marys
Junior School
AV
Popes Row
Kingshill
Primary School
Vallans
The Cl
Clifton
Kingsway
PO
Cheyne Way
Redan Rd
Hither Fld
Clarks Cl
Horrocks Close
Fanhams Road
Coltsfoot Road
Larksfield
Grsmr Rd
Great Cozens
Hall Road
Linwood Road
Rshf Rd
Elder Road
Chestnut Avenue
Ash Road
Evergreen Road
Priors Wood JMI School

2

Milton Road
Thund
Derout
Bourne Cl
Southill
Cl
High
Homefield Rd
Oak Rd
Quaker Rd
Hill
Tower
Road
Redan Rd
Western House Hosp
Musley Infant School
Fanhams Road
Cundells Rd
Queens Rd
Sells Rd
Parnel Road
Beechfield Road
Grove Rd
Woodley Road
Beacon Road
Elms Road

15

3

The Bourne
Collett Road
Lime Cl
Musley Hill
Trinity Road
kg George Rd
PO
WARE
Cobham Rd
Cozens
The Vineyard

Princes Street
Coronation
Francis Rd
Church Street Ind Estate
Deerfield Close
Hanbury Close
New Road
Musley Lane
Kiln House
Grantham Gdns
Kg Edward's Rd
George
Hampde Hill
H H Cl
Popis Cotts
Upper Clabdens
Cromwell
Uplands
Lwr Clabdens

16

Surgery
Church St
East St
Kibes La
Christ Church Primary School
Bowling
Clements Road
Vicarage Rd
Cross St
Garland Rd
Raynsford Rd
Musley La
Win V Rd
Vicarage Rd
Barley Ponds Road
Ltl Widbury Lane

HIGH ST
ers Coll
West St
Surgery
STAR ST
B1004
Works
Ms Mn
Ltl Widbury Lane

4

Broadmeads
PO
LGt
AMWELL END
Station
River
Ware Station
Works
Mill Studio Business Centre
Crane Mead
WIDBURY HILL
B1004

214

-FORD ROAD
Middleton Rd
Scott's Rd
Scotts
Hertford Regional College
LONDON RD
VIADUCT RD
A119
A119
Grange Gdns
Presdales Dr
Marsh Lane
Hollycross Road

5

er Grotto Road
cres
Cedar
Walton
Hoe Lane
Windmill Fld
Presdales School
Gilpin Rd
Red House Close
Presdales Dr
Peters Wd
LONDON ROAD
A1170
Works
Lea Valley Walk
River Lee Navigation

E F **25** G H

36 37

Presdales

Pinewood Special

Yearling

16

A   B   C   D

5 38   39

Babbs Green

Kingham Rd

New Hall Farm

Noah's Ark

1

Fanhams Hall

16

Harcamlow Way

Wareside Primary School

2

Morley Hall

15

3

◄ **15**

Harcamlow Way

B1004

Harcamlow Way

Mardocks Farm

4

B1004

214

Watersplace Farm

5

5 38   39

Easneye

A   B   ▼ **26**   C   D

All Nations Christian College

1 grid square represents 500 metres

Blakesware
Manor

E   F   G   H

40   41

Hertfordshire

Ash

Helham
Green

Scholar's   Hill

Scholar's   Hill

B1004

B1004   WARE ROAD

Widford J
Infant Sch

Hertfordshire   Way

B1004

1

B1004

Ab

Wareside

Hertfordshire   Way

16

2

River Ash

15

WIDFORD ROAD

3

Hunsdon

Paddock
Close

Fillets
Farm

Chestnut Close

4

PO

Tanners

214

Tudor Cl

St D Rd

Harcamlow Way

Rectory
Close

Harcamlow   Way

Way

5

Newgate
Wood

Harcamlow Way

Acorn

Spe

E   F   **27**   G   H

40   41

B180

Bonningtons

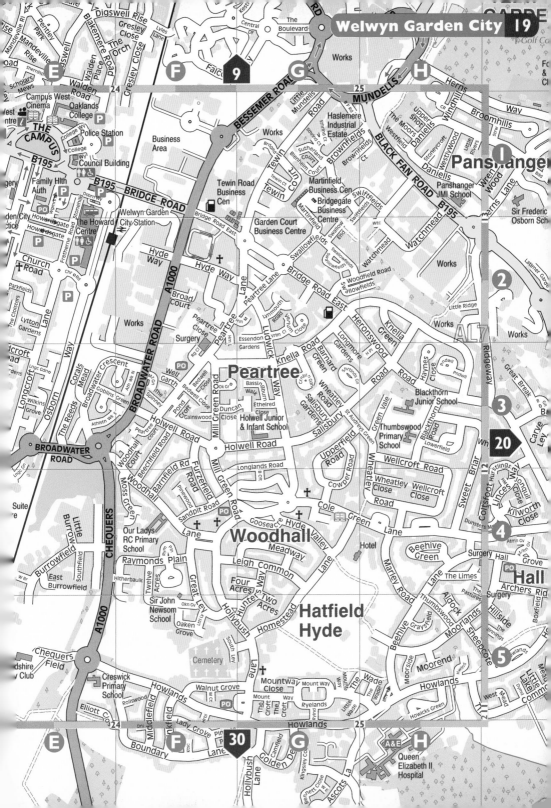

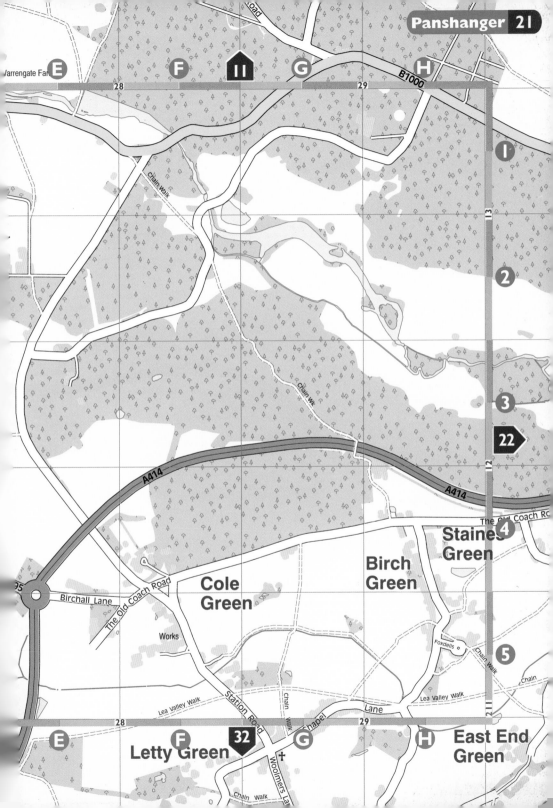

Warrengate Far **E**   **F**   **II**   **G**   B1000   **H**

28   29   **I**

13

Chain Walk

2

3

Chain Wlk

22

12

A414   A414

The Old Coach Rd

Staines Green

4

Birch Green

95   Birchall Lane   The Old Coach Road   **Cole Green**

Works

Foxdells   Chain Walk

5

Chain

Lea Valley Walk   Lea Valley Walk

28   Station Road   Chapel   Lane   29

E   **F**   **32**   **G**   **H**   **East End Green**

Letty Green   Woolmers La   Chain Walk

chain Walk

E **Newgate Wood** F **17** G H

40 41

Harcamlow Way

Harcamlow Way

B180

Bonningtons

Works

Hunsdonbury

Acorn St

Spe

I

Halfway House

HUNSDON ROAD

B180

Olives Farm

2

B180

Home Farm Industrial Estate

Lord's Wood

3

Harcamlow Way

4

A414

Golf Course

Briggen

5

Stanstead Lodge

Briggens House Hotel Golf Club

E F G H

40 41

Harcamlow Way

Hertfor

A 5 20 **B** **C** 21 **D**

I

Symondshyde Great Wood

2 Coopers Green Lane

3 Cooper's
Green

Coopers Green Lane

Astwick
Manor

School of Art
& Design

Hatfield
Business
Park

Frobisher Way

Hatfield Avenue

**Hatfie
Villag**

Gre

4

Hatfield
Aerodrome

5

Bishops Squ
Business Pa

Ellenbrook

A 5 20 **B** **C** 21 **D**

A1057

ST ALBANS ROAD WEST

St Albans Road West

Hatfield

30

Chequers Field

Hertfordshire Country Club

Creswick Primary School

Cemetery

Ryde

Beeh

Moorend

The Wade

Moorside

Howlands

A
Elliott
Rolliswood
Middlefield
Linkfield
Howl
Walnut Gre

B
Lady Grove
Boundary
Lane
Kendall
Pinnate Place
KRSC
dry

19
The Croft
Mount
The Croft
elands

C
Mountway Close
Mount Way
Camfield
Golden Dell
Kingsley Court
Hollybush Lane
Bechert Close
W m

Howlands

D
The Wade
Little Wade
Howicks Green

A & E
Queen Elizabeth II Hospital

I
Walk

Woodhall Farm

Ascots Lane
Golf Course

Ascots La

Gypsy Lane

2

Lea Valley Walk
Mill Green Lane

Mill Green Golf Club

A414

Hotel
CHEQUERS

Mount Pleasant Cl
Mount Pleasant
Lane
The Ryde
High
The Ryde
Green Avenue
Lodge Drive
SunnyField
The Holdings
Greenfield
The Ryde Primary School
Bush Hall Lane

MILL GREEN

Lea Valley Walk

Home Park

The Vineyard

A414

3

29
Industrial area
The Ryde
Fawn Cl

The Ryde

Ryde View
Park View
Burleigh Mead

4
ROAD EAST

HERTFORD ROAD
Old Hertford Road

HERTFORD ROAD

A1000

Park Meadow
Street
09

P
Hatfield Station

5

PO
Park Cl
Park

Batterdale
Fore Street
Church Street
Church Lane
The Broadway

Old Hatfield

A
Hatfield House

Real Tennis Club

B

36

C

D

1 grid square represents 500 metres

Commonswood
JMI School

E **F** **20** **G** **H**

26 27

Holwell Hyde Lane

Burnside

HATFIELD ROAD

A414

Holwell Court

1

2

Lea Valley Walk

HERTFORD ROAD

HOLWELL LANE

B1455

River Lea or Lee

Lea Valley Walk

Lea Valley Walk

Essendonbury
Farm

LOW ROAD

3

32

4

ESSENDON HILL B158 209

Church
St

5

Rectory Cl

Glb Cl

Glebe Cottages

East View

School Lane

E **F** **37** **West End** **G** **H**

26 27

End Lane

HIGH ROAD

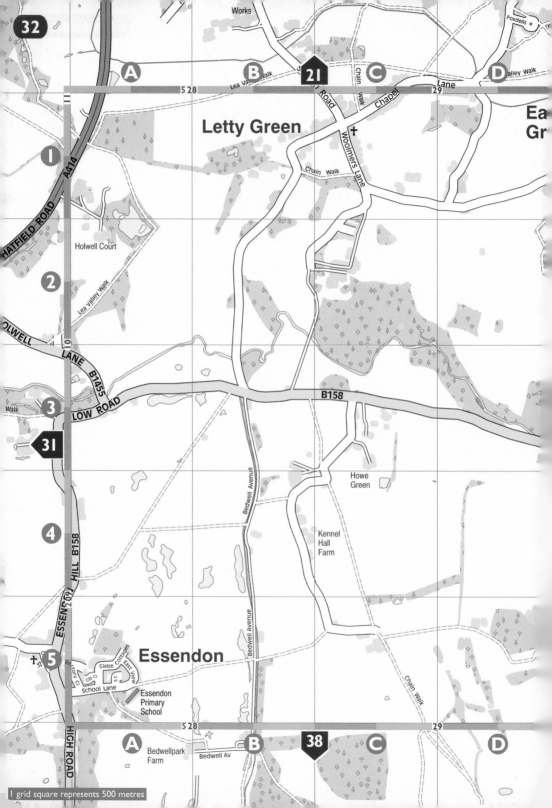

32

A 5 28 **B** Lea Valley Walk **21** **C** Chain Walk Lane 29 **D** Valley Walk

Works

Foxdells

1

Letty Green

Ea
Gr

HATFIELD ROAD A414

Chapel

Woolmers Lane

Chain Walk

2

Holwell Court

Lea valley walk

OLWELL

LANE

B1455

3

Walk

LOW ROAD

B158

31

Bedwell Avenue

Howe
Green

4

Kennel
Hall
Farm

ESSENDON HILL B158

5

Essendon

Glebe Cottages
Rectory Cl East View
Gro Cl C S
School Lane

Essendon
Primary
School

Chain Walk

HIGH ROAD

A 5 28 **B** Bedwell Av **38** **C** 29 **D**

Bedwellpark
Farm

E   F   **22**   G   H

30   31

I

Bayfordbury
Park Farm

Lea or Lee

HATFIELD

ROAD

Roxford

LOWER

Bayfordbury
College of
Hertfordshire

2

LOWER HATFIELD ROAD

Works

Broad Green

Broad Green
Wood

**Broadgreen
Wood**

3

Water Hall
Farm

Chain

Walk

Bayford Lane

4

SG13

Bayford
Hall

Chain Walk

Culverwood
House

Warren House

†

Bayford Green

Well-Row

5

209

Stockings Lane

30

E   F   **39**   G   **Bayford**   H

31

Bayford
Wood

Bayford
Primary
School

Bayford
Station

ne Road

36
PO

Park
Park Cl

Batterdale
Broadway
Church Street
Church Lane
Fore Street

Old Hatfield

A   B   **30**   C   D

5 24   25

Real Tennis Club

Hatfield House

I

Coombe Wood

Park Dairy

2

3

35

4

Millward's Park

Woodside Place

Woo

Wildhill Road

Woodside Lane

A1000

Marshmoor

AL9

Woodside

Lower Woodside

5

Travellers'

Works

Marshmoor Crs

Works
Travellers Cl

Alpha Business Park

A   The Rookery   B   **42**   C   Westfield Lane   D

5 24   25

Welham Green Station

Marshmoor Lane

A1000

GREAT

West End

E F 31 G H

26 27

School Lane

HIGH ROAD

I

Golf

80

Essendon Place

2

Bedwe Park
Hatfiel Count

Pope's Farm

B158

3

38

Camfield Place

207

Cucumber Hall Farm

Wildhill

4

KENTISH LANE

Hornbeam Lane

Warrenwood Park

5

Woodhill House

206

E F 43 G H

26 27

Woodfield Lane

Grubbs Lane

Woodfield Farm

38

Essendon

Rectory Cl
Glebe Cottages
GtD Cl
East View
School Lane

A Essendon
Primary
School

HIGH ROAD

B

Bedwell

32

Chain Walk

C

D

5 28

29

Bedwellpark
Farm

Bedwell Av

1

Golf Course

80

Essendon
Place

2

Bedwell
Park
Hatfield London
Country Club

Little Berkhamstead La

Church Road

Goddards

**Little
Berkhamsted**

Chain Walk

Little   Berkhamstead   Lane

3

B158

Bedwell Lodge
Farm

37

207

Cucumber Hall
Farm

Cucumber Lane

4

Woodcock
Lodge

Epp
Hou
Sch

5

206

**Tylers
Causeway**

Chain Walk

Woodcock Lodge
Farm

Tylers Causeway

5 28

29

A

Woodfield Lane

B

C

D

1 grid square represents 500 metres

Culverwood
House

E **F** **33** ford **G** Well-Row Bayford **H**
Wood

30 31

Bayford

Bayford
Primary
School

Stockings Lane

Bayford
Station

I

Ashendene Road

Chain Walk

08

Bucks

Alley

2 Brick
Gra
Golf

Bucks
Farm

Ponsbourne
Tunnel

Blackfan
Wood

3

07

Ashendene
Farm

Chain Walk

Old Claypits
Farm

4

pping
reen

5

206

Path short valley Way

30 31

E **F** **G** **H**

Ponsbourne

40

TH ORBITAL ROAD

A414

Green

Jun

St Marks Ct

Church Lane

High St

Wistlea Crs

Richards Cl

Cuthmore

PI

Colney Heath JM&I School

Colney
Heath
34

Roestock Lane

Franklin Close

Roestock Gardens

Green

D

Jun

A

Park Corner

Heathside

5 20

Park La

PO

B

High

Street

C

Roestock Lane

Hall Gardens

Roestock

Bullen's

21

I

06

Coursers Rd

Meadway

a Cl

Admirals Close

Fellowes Lane

Dll La

Tolle
Far

2

05

Warren Farm

River Colne

Tollgate Road

Tyttenhanger Farm

3

Coursers Road

Coursers Farm

4

204

's Road

5

204

Walsingham Wood

Junction 22

5 20

21

A

B

C

D

Cobs Ash

1 grid square represents 500 metres

E
F
35
G
H

Travellers

Bishops Rise

Cemetery

Works
Marshmoor Crs

Dellsome Lane

Pooleys Lane

Works
Travellers Cl

Marshmoor Lane

Welham Gr Station

Welham Green Station

Parsonage Road
Frowick

Parsonage Lane
Huggins Lane
Puttocks Drive

Alpha Business Park

Hill Road

I

St Marys Primary School

B C

Vincenzo Close

Dixons

Nash Close
Booths Close

Welham Green

Merritt Wk
Dellsome Lane

Somers Road

Holloways Lane

Skimpans Close

Gould Close
Knolles Crescent
Greville Cl
A C
PO
Grv Pl
Welham Cl

Lydia Mews

Meadow

2

Welham Manor

Station Rd

3 Potterells Medical Centre

A1(M)

Dixons Hill Close

Dixons Hill Road

42

Tollgate Road

North Mymms Cricket Club

Water End

4 Bradmore

A204

Swanland Road

Abdale Lane

5

E
F
G
H

Warrengate Road

New Cottages

Royal Colle

AL9

A   B   36 ower Woodside   C   D

524   25

Travellers
Works
Works
Travellers Cl
Alpha Business Park
Marshmoor Crs
Marshmoor Lane
Welham Green Station
Hill Road
Holloways Lane
Dixons
Nash Close
Booths Close
Somers Road
S Sq
Welham Cl
Lydia Mews
Cnng
Rd
Skimpans Close
Meadow Cl
Sb Rd
The Rookery
Woodside
Westfield Lane
Grub

A1000
GREAT NORTH ROAD

1

Fox's Lane

2

Bulls Lane

Bell Lane

B
B

Ash Close

Station Road

3

Potterells Medical Centre
Potterells

4 1

Brookmans Park Golf Club

Golf Course
Golf Club Road

Peplins Way
Brookmans Park Primary School
Peplins Way
Peplins Way
Peplins Cl
Bradmore Way

Brookmans Park

4

Bradmore Lane

Green Cl
St Cl
PO
Bradmore Green
Surgery
The Close
Brookmans Lane
Avenue
Park Close
Moffats Close

†

The Grove

5

Brookmans Park Station
Westland Drive
Oaklands Avenue
Blue Bridge Road
Moffats Close
Bluebridge Avenue

The Gardens

A al Veterinary College
B   C   D

524   25

90   204   05

E
F
37 dhill House
G
H

26
27
06

Woodfield Lane

I

Grubbs Lane

†

Woodfield Farm

Barbers Lodge Farm

Kentish Lane Farm

KENTISH LANE

2

B158

05

hancellors chool

Pine

Upland

Grove

Drive

Great North Road

3

Wood Road

4

Shrublands

Woodlands

04

Avenue

Calder Av

Woodlands

Drive

B157

SHEPHERDS WAY

Ramsey Cl

Woodlands

5

ions ood

E
F
Queenswood School
G
H

26
27

Well V

Swanley ar

A1000

GREAT

Ayot Green	8 A5	Datchworth Green	5 F1
Ayot St Lawrence	2 A4	Digswell	9 G2
Ayot St Peter	8 A2	Digswell Park	9 E4
Babbs Green	16 C1	Digswell Water	9 H3
Bayford	39 G1	East End Green	32 D1
Bell Bar	42 D2	Ellenbrook	28 C5
Bengeo	13 E5	Epping Green	39 E5
Birch Green	21 H4	Essendon	32 A5
Birchwood	29 G4	The Frythe	8 B3
Bramfield	11 H1	Great Amwell	25 F3
Broadgreen Wood	33 H3	Haldens	9 H3
Broadoak End	12 C5	Hall Grove	20 A4
Brookmans Park	42 B4	Handside	18 C3
Bullen's Green	34 D5	Harmer Green	4 D5
Bull's Green	5 G3	Hartham	23 F1
Burnham Green	5 F4	Hatfield	35 E2
Codicote	3 E1	Hatfield Garden Village	28 D3
Codicote Bottom	2 C2	Hatfield Hyde	19 G5
Cold Christmas	7 H4	Helham Green	17 E1
Cole Green	21 F4	Hertford	23 H3
Colney Heath	34 B5	Hertford Heath	24 C5
Cooper's Green	28 A3	Hertingfordbury	22 D3
Danesbury	3 H4	Hunsdon	17 H4
Hunsdonbury	27 H2	South Hatfield	35 G4
Lemsford	18 A3	Staines Green	21 H4
Letty Green	32 B1	Stanborough	18 A5
Little Berkamstead	38 B2	Stanstead Abbotts	26 D4
Lower Woodside	36 C5	Tewin	10 D3
Marshmoor	36 A5	Tewin Wood	5 G5
Mill Green	30 B3	Thundridge	7 F3
Nast Hyde	34 C2	Tonwell	6 A3
Oaklands	4 D3	Tylers Causeway	38 C5
Old Hatfield	30 A5	Wadesmill	7 E2
Oxlease	35 G2	Ware	15 G5
Panshanger	19 H1	Wareside	17 E2
Peartree	19 F3	Water End	41 H4
Pottersheath	3 H1	Waterford	12 C3
Presdales	25 F1	Welham Green	41 G1
Roe Green	35 F1	Welwyn	3 F5
Roestock	40 C1	Welwyn Garden City	10 A5
Rush Green	24 D2	West End	37 G1
The Ryde	29 H3	Wildhill	37 F4
St Margarets	25 H4	Woodhall	19 F4
Sherrardspark	8 C5	Woodside	36 D4
Sleapshyde	34 B4	Youngsbury	7 G2
Smallford	34 A2		

USING THE STREET INDEX

Street names are listed alphabetically. Each street name is followed by its postal town or area locality, the Postcode District, the page number, and the reference to the square in which the name is found.

Standard index entries are shown as follows:

Abbots Cl *KNEB* SG3............................**5** G1

Street names and selected addresses not shown on the map due to scale restrictions are shown in the index with an asterisk:

Albany Rd *WGCE* * AL7 ....**19** F2

GENERAL ABBREVIATIONS

ACC	ACCESS	E	EAST	LDG	LODGE	R	RIVER
ALY	ALLEY	EMB	EMBANKMENT	LGT	LIGHT	RBT	ROUNDABOUT
AP	APPROACH	EMBY	EMBASSY	LK	LOCK	RD	ROAD
AR	ARCADE	ESP	ESPLANADE	LKS	LAKES	RDG	RIDGE
ASS	ASSOCIATION	EST	ESTATE	LNDG	LANDING	REP	REPUBLIC
AV	AVENUE	EX	EXCHANGE	LTL	LITTLE	RES	RESERVOIR
BCH	BEACH	EXPY	EXPRESSWAY	LWR	LOWER	RFC	RUGBY FOOTBALL CLUB
BLDS	BUILDINGS	EXT	EXTENSION	MAG	MAGISTRATE	RI	RISE
BND	BEND	F/O	FLYOVER	MAN	MANSIONS	RP	RAMP
BNK	BANK	FC	FOOTBALL CLUB	MD	MEAD	RW	ROW
BR	BRIDGE	FK	FORK	MDW	MEADOWS	S	SOUTH
BRK	BROOK	FLD	FIELD	MEM	MEMORIAL	SCH	SCHOOL
BTM	BOTTOM	FLDS	FIELDS	MKT	MARKET	SE	SOUTH EAST
BUS	BUSINESS	FLS	FALLS	MKTS	MARKETS	SER	SERVICE AREA
BVD	BOULEVARD	FLS	FLATS	ML	MALL	SH	SHORE
BY	BYPASS	FM	FARM	ML	MILL	SHOP	SHOPPING
CATH	CATHEDRAL	FT	FORT	MNR	MANOR	SKWY	SKYWAY
CEM	CEMETERY	FWY	FREEWAY	MS	MEWS	SMT	SUMMIT
CEN	CENTRE	FY	FERRY	MSN	MISSION	SOC	SOCIETY
CFT	CROFT	GA	GATE	MT	MOUNT	SP	SPUR
CH	CHURCH	GAL	GALLERY	MTN	MOUNTAIN	SPR	SPRING
CHA	CHASE	GDN	GARDEN	MTS	MOUNTAINS	SQ	SQUARE
CHYD	CHURCHYARD	GDNS	GARDENS	MUS	MUSEUM	ST	STREET
CIR	CIRCLE	GLD	GLADE	MWY	MOTORWAY	STN	STATION
CIRC	CIRCUS	GLN	GLEN	N	NORTH	STR	STREAM
CL	CLOSE	GN	GREEN	NE	NORTH EAST	STRD	STRAND
CLFS	CLIFFS	GND	GROUND	NW	NORTH WEST	SW	SOUTH WEST
CMP	CAMP	GRA	GRANGE	O/P	OVERPASS	TDG	TRADING
CNR	CORNER	GRG	GARAGE	OFF	OFFICE	TER	TERRACE
CO	COUNTY	GT	GREAT	ORCH	ORCHARD	THWY	THROUGHWAY
COLL	COLLEGE	GTWY	GATEWAY	OV	OVAL	TNL	TUNNEL
COM	COMMON	GV	GROVE	PAL	PALACE	TOLL	TOLLWAY
COMM	COMMISSION	HGR	HIGHER	PAS	PASSAGE	TPK	TURNPIKE
CON	CONVENT	HL	HILL	PAV	PAVILION	TR	TRACK
COT	COTTAGE	HLS	HILLS	PDE	PARADE	TRL	TRAIL
COTS	COTTAGES	HO	HOUSE	PH	PUBLIC HOUSE	TWR	TOWER
CP	CAPE	HOL	HOLLOW	PK	PARK	U/P	UNDERPASS
CPS	COPSE	HOSP	HOSPITAL	PKWY	PARKWAY	UNI	UNIVERSITY
CR	CREEK	HRB	HARBOUR	PL	PLACE	UPR	UPPER
CREM	CREMATORIUM	HTH	HEATH	PLN	PLAIN	V	VALE
CRS	CRESCENT	HTS	HEIGHTS	PLNS	PLAINS	VA	VALLEY
CSWY	CAUSEWAY	HVN	HAVEN	PLZ	PLAZA	VIAD	VIADUCT
CT	COURT	HWY	HIGHWAY	POL	POLICE STATION	VIL	VILLA
CTRL	CENTRAL	IMP	IMPERIAL	PR	PRINCE	VIS	VISTA
CTS	COURTS	IN	INLET	PREC	PRECINCT	VLG	VILLAGE
CTYD	COURTYARD	IND EST	INDUSTRIAL ESTATE	PREP	PREPARATORY	VLS	VILLAS
CUTT	CUTTINGS	INF	INFIRMARY	PRIM	PRIMARY	VW	VIEW
CV	COVE	INFO	INFORMATION	PROM	PROMENADE	W	WEST
CYN	CANYON	INT	INTERCHANGE	PRS	PRINCESS	WD	WOOD
DEPT	DEPARTMENT	IS	ISLAND	PRT	PORT	WHF	WHARF
DL	DALE	JCT	JUNCTION	PT	POINT	WK	WALK
DM	DAM	JTY	JETTY	PTH	PATH	WKS	WALKS
DR	DRIVE	KG	KING	PZ	PIAZZA	WLS	WELLS
DRO	DROVE	KNL	KNOLL	QD	QUADRANT	WY	WAY
DRY	DRIVEWAY	L	LAKE	QU	QUEEN	YD	YARD
DWGS	DWELLINGS	LA	LANE	QY	QUAY	YHA	YOUTH HOSTEL

POSTCODE TOWNS AND AREA ABBREVIATIONS

BRKMPK..............................Brookmans Park
HAT...Hatfield
HERT/BAY.....................Hertford/Bayford
HERT/WAT.........Hertford/Watton at Stone

HTCHE/RSTV ....Hitchin east/
Rural Stevenage
KNEB................................Knebworth
POTB/CUF.................Potters Bar/Cuffley

STALE/WH ....St Albans east/
Wheathampstead
STDN..Standon
WARE...Ware

WGCE ....Welwyn Garden City east
WGCW..................Welwyn Garden City west
WLYN ....Welwyn

Index - streets

Abb - Chr

A

Abbots Cl *KNEB* SG3.............5 G1
Abbotts Ri *WARE* SG12.....26 C4
Abbotts Wy *WARE* SG12.....26 C4
Abdale La *BRKMPK* AL9....41 G5
Acacia St *HAT* AL10.........35 F4
Acorn Gld *WLYN* AL6..........9 G1
Adele Av *WLYN* AL6............9 G2
Admirals Cl *STALE/WH* AL4....40 D1
Admiral St *HERT/BAY* SG13....24 B2
Albany Rd *WGCE* * AL7.......19 F2
Alconbury Gv *WGCE* AL7.....20 D2
Aldbury Gv *WGCE* AL7.......20 A2
Alderman Cl *BRKMPK* AL9....41 H2
Aldock *WGCE* AL7............19 H4
Aldwyke Ri *WARE* SG12.....14 D2
Alldykes *HAT* AL10..........35 E1
Alexander Rd *HERT/WAS* SG14....22 D2
Allen Ct *HAT* * AL10.........35 G3
Amberley Gn *WARE* SG12....14 D1
Amwell Common *WGCE* AL7....20 A3
Amwell End *WARE* SG12.....15 E5
Amwell Hl *WARE* SG12......25 G2
Amwell La *WARE* SG12......25 H2
Anchor La *WARE* SG12........6 C4
Andrewsfield *WGCE* AL7.....20 D2
Apex Point *BRKMPK* * AL9....35 H5
Applecroft Rd *WGCW* AL8....18 C2
Apple Arbour *HERT/BAY* SG13....23 G4
Archers Cl *HERT/WAS* SG14....23 F1
Archers Green La *WLYN* AL6....10 C5
Archers Ride *WARE* AL7.....20 A4
Archfield *WGCE* AL7...........9 F4
Arcots La *BRKMPK* AL9......30 B2
Arlbury Cl *HAT* AL10.........34 D1
Arn Cl *BRKMPK* AL9..........42 D3
Arncombe *WGCW* AL8..........9 F3
Arn Dr *HAT* AL10.............35 F4
Arnendene Rd *HERT/BAY* SG13....39 G1
Arnley Cl *WGCW* AL8...........8 D5
Arnley Rd *HERT/WAS* SG14....22 D2
Arn Rd *WARE* SG12...........15 H2
Aspen Wy *WGCE* AL7..........29 E3
Astwick Av *HAT* AL10.........29 E3
Athelstan Wk North *WGCE* AL7....19 F3
Athelstan Wk South *WGCE* AL7....19 E3
Atmore Cl *WGCW* AL8.........18 C3
Atrimore Rd *WGCW* AL8.......18 C3
Autumn Gv *WGCE* AL7........20 A4
Avenue Ct *WLYN* AL6...........4 B3
The Avenue *HERT/WAS* SG14....13 E5
WLYN AL6......................4 A3
Avent Gn *WGCW* AL8...........8 A4
Avent Little Green La *WLYN* AL6....8 A4

B

Back La *WLYN* AL6...........10 D3
Baker Cl *WGCE* AL7..........20 B2
Ballingers Cl *HERT/BAY* SG13....24 C2
Ballingers Wk *WLYN* AL6......5 F5
Balmoor Wy *HAT* AL10........20 B1
Balmer's La *WLYN* AL6.........3 H4
Balmer St *HERT/BAY* SG13....23 H2
Bancock St *WARE* SG12.......15 E3
Bandwins *WGCE* AL7..........20 A2
Balmour St *HERT/WAS* SG14....23 F1
Balrams Cl *HERT/BAY* SG13....23 G4
Baraville Camp
BRKMPK * AL9................30 C3
Barclay Cl *HERT/BAY* SG13....24 C4
Barkley Cft *HERT/WAS* SG14....13 G5
HERT/WAS SG14................13 G5
Barleycroft Rd *WGCE* AL7......6 A3
Barleycroft Gn *WGCW* AL8....18 D2
Barleywood Rd *WGCW* AL8....18 D3
Barley Ponds Cl *WARE* SG12....15 G4
Barley Ponds Rd *WARE* SG12....15 G4
Barnard Gn *WGCE* AL7.......19 G3
Barn Cl *WGCW* AL8...........18 D2

Barndicott *WGCE* AL7........20 B2
Barnfield Rd *WGCE* AL7......19 F4
Barnside Ct *WGCW* AL8......18 D2
Bartletts Md *HERT/WAS* SG14....13 G4
Bassingburn Wk *WGCE* AL7....19 C3
Batford Cl *WGCE* AL7........20 A3
Batterdale *BRKMPK* AL9.....29 H5
Bayford Cl *HERT/BAY* SG13....23 H4
Bayford Gn *HERT/BAY* SG13....33 H5
Bayford La *HERT/BAY* SG13....33 G3
Beacon Ct *HERT/BAY* * SG13....24 D5
Beacon Rd *WARE* SG12.......15 H3
Beaconsfield Ct *HAT* * AL10....29 H4
Beaconsfield Rd *HAT* AL10....29 H5
Beane River Vw
HERT/WAS SG14................23 F2
Beane Rd *HERT/WAS* SG14....23 E2
Beatham Ct *WARE* * SG12....13 H1
Beazley Ct *WARE* SG12......15 F3
Becket Gdns *WLYN* AL6......15 E2
Beckets Wk *WARE* * SG12....15 E4
Becketts *HERT/WAS* SG14....22 D3
Bedwell Av *BRKMPK* AL9.....38 B1
HERT/BAY SG13................32 B4
Bedwell Cl *WGCE* AL7........19 F3
Beech Cl *HAT* AL10..........35 F4
Beechfield Rd *WARE* SG12....15 C3
WGCE AL7......................19 F4
Beech Ms *WARE* SG12.......25 E1
Beechwood Cl *HERT/BAY* SG13....24 A2
Beehive Gn *WGCE* AL7.......19 H4
Beehive La *WGCE* AL7.......19 H5
Belle Vue Rd *WARE* SG12....15 F4
Bell La *BRKMPK* AL9.........42 D2
HERT/WAS SG14................23 F2
Bengeo Mdw *HERT/WAS* * SG14....13 F4
Bengeo Ms *HERT/WAS* * SG14....13 F4
Bengeo St *HERT/WAS* SG14....23 F1
Bennett Cl *BRKMPK* AL9.....30 C1
Bennetts Cl *STALE/WH* AL4....40 C1
Bentley Rd *HERT/WAS* SG14....22 B1
Bericot Wy *WGCE* AL7.......20 B2
Berkeley Cl *WARE* SG12.....14 D3
Bessemer Rd *WGCW* AL8......9 F3
Beverley Gdns *WGCE* AL7....20 B2
Birchall La *HERT/WAS* SG14....20 C6
Birchall Wd *WGCE* AL7.......20 B3
Birch Dr *HAT* AL10..........35 F2
Bircherley Ct *HERT/WAS* * SG14....23 G2
Bircherley St *HERT/WAS* SG14....23 G2
The Birches *WLYN* AL6.......3 E2
Birch Gv *WLYN* AL6...........6 B2
Birch Rd *KNEB* SG3...........5 E1
Birchway *HAT* AL10..........29 F4
Birchwood Av *HAT* AL10.....29 F4
Birchwood Cl *HAT* AL10.....29 F4
Birdcroft Rd *WGCW* AL8.....19 E3
Birdie Wy *HERT/BAY* SG13....24 C1
Birds Cl *WGCE* AL7..........20 A4
Bishops Cl *HAT* AL10.........35 E1
Bishops Ri *HAT* AL10........35 E2
Bishops Rd *WLYN* AL6.........5 G4
Black Fan Rd *WGCE* AL7......19 G1
Black Smiths Cl *WARE* SG12....25 H1
Black Swan Ct *WARE* * SG12....15 E4
Blackthorne Cl *HAT* AL10....35 E4
Blackthorn Rd *WGCE* AL7....19 H3
Blakemere Rd *WGCW* AL8......9 E5
Blakes Wy *WLYN* AL6.........5 H4
The Blanes *WARE* SG12......14 D2
Blenheim Cl *WGCE* AL7......19 F2
Blenheim Ct *WGCE* * AL7.....19 G1
Bluebell Cl *HERT/BAY* SG13....24 B2
Bluebells *WLYN* AL6...........4 B3
Bluebridge Av *BRKMPK* AL9....42 B5
Blue Bridge Rd *BRKMPK* AL9....42 B5
Bluecoats Av *HERT/WAS* SG14....23 C2
Bluecoat Yd *WARE* SG12.....15 E4
Blythway *WGCE* AL7...........9 C4
Booths Cl *BRKMPK* AL9......42 A2
The Boulevard *WGCE* AL7.....9 C5
Boundary Dr *HERT/WAS* SG14....13 H5
Boundary La *WGCE* AL7......30 B1
Bourne Cl *WARE* SG12.......15 E2
The Bourne *WARE* SG12......15 E3
Bowling Rd *WARE* SG12......15 F4

Bowmans Cl *WLYN* AL6........3 H3
Boxfield *WGCE* AL7..........20 A5
Bracken La *WLYN* AL6.........4 C3
Bradmore Gn *BRKMPK* AL9....42 B4
Bradmore La *BRKMPK* AL9....42 A4
Bradmore Wy *BRKMPK* AL9....42 B4
Bradshaws *HAT* AL10.........35 E5
Brain Cl *HAT* AL10...........29 G5
Bramble Rd *HAT* AL10.......34 B2
The Brambles *WARE* SG12....14 D2
WLYN AL6.......................4 B2
Bramfield La *HERT/WAS* SG14....12 B2
Bramfield Rd *HERT/WAS* SG14....12 B5
KNEB SG14.....................5 C1
Branch Cl *HAT* AL10.........29 H4
Braziers Fld *HERT/BAY* SG13....24 A2
Breakmead *WGCE* AL7........20 A4
Breaks Rd *HAT* AL10.........35 G1
Brewhouse La *HERT/WAS* SG14....23 F2
Briardale *WARE* SG12........14 D2
Briars Cl *HAT* AL10..........35 F1
Briars La *HAT* AL10..........35 F1
The Briars *HERT/BAY* SG13....24 B2
Briars Wd *HAT* AL10.........35 F1
Briary Wood End *WLYN* AL6....4 C2
Briary Wood La *WLYN* AL6.....4 C2
Brickendon La *HERT/BAY* SG13....23 F5
Brickfield *HAT* AL10.........35 F4
The Brickfields *WARE* SG12....14 C3
Brickwall Cl *WGCW* AL8.......8 B5
Bridgefields *WGCE* AL7......19 G1
Bridge Foot *WARE* * SG12....15 E4
Bridge Rd *WGCE* AL7.........18 D1
Bridge Rd East *WGCE* AL7....19 F1
Bridges Ct *HERT/WAS* SG14....23 F2
Bridle Wy *WARE* SG12.......25 H2
Broad Acres *HAT* AL10......29 E3
Broad Ct *WGCE* AL7..........19 F2
Broadfield Pl *WGCW* AL8....18 C3
Broadfield Rd *KNEB* SG3.....5 E1
Broad Gn *HERT/BAY* SG13....33 G3
Broad Green Wd
HERT/BAY SG13................33 G3
Broadleaf Gv *WGCE* AL6......8 C4
Broadmeads *WARE* SG12.....15 E4
Broadoak End
HERT/WAS * SG14.............12 C4
Broadwater Crs *WGCE* AL7....19 E3
Broadwater Rd *WGCE* AL7....19 F3
The Broadway *BRKMPK* AL9....35 H1
Brocket Rd *WGCW* AL8.......18 C3
Brockett Cl *WGCW* AL8......18 C2
Brockswood La *WGCW* AL8....18 C1
Brookmans Av *BRKMPK* AL9....42 C4
Brooks Ct *HERT/WAS* * SG14....22 C1
Brooksfield *WGCE* AL7.......20 A1
Brookside *HAT* AL10.........34 C1
HERT/BAY SG13................23 H3
Broom Cl *HAT* AL10..........35 E4
Broomfield Cl *WLYN* AL6......8 D1
Broomfield Rd *WLYN* AL6......8 D1
Broom Hl *WLYN* AL6...........4 D2
Broomhills *WGCE* AL7........19 H1
Brooms Cl *WGCW* AL8........9 E4
Brownfields *WGCE* AL7......19 G1
Brownfields Ct *WGCE* AL7....19 G1
Bryce Cl *WARE* SG12........15 E2
Bucks Aly *HERT/BAY* SG13....39 E2
Buddcroft *WGCE* AL7........20 A1
Bullen's Green La
STALE/WH AL4.................40 D1
Bullock's La *HERT/BAY* SG13....23 F4
Bull Pln *HERT/WAS* SG14....23 G2
Bullrush Cl *HAT* AL10.......35 G2
Bulls La *BRKMPK* AL9........42 B2
Bull Stag Gn *BRKMPK* AL9....29 H4
Bunnsfield *WGCE* AL7........20 B2
Burfield Cl *HAT* AL10.......35 E4
Burgage Ct *WARE* * SG12....15 E4
Burgundy Cft *WGCE* AL7.....19 G4
Burleigh Md *BRKMPK* AL9....29 H4
Burleigh Rd *HERT/WAS* SG14....24 B1
Burnett Sq *HERT/WAS* SG14....22 C1
Burnham Cl *WLYN* AL6........5 F4
Burnham Green Rd *WLYN* AL6....5 G4
Burnside *HERT/WAS* SG14....22 D3

C

Burrowfield *WGCE* AL7......19 E4
Burycroft *WGCW* AL8..........9 F4
Buryfield Wy *WARE* SG12....14 D3
Bury La *HERT/WAS* SG14.....11 G1
WLYN AL6.......................3 E1
Bury Rd *HAT* AL10...........29 H5
Bushey Cl *WGCE* AL7........20 A3
Bushey Gn *WGCE* AL7........20 A3
Bushey Ley *WGCE* AL7.......20 A3
Bush Hall La *BRKMPK* AL9....30 A3
Bushwood Cl *BRKMPK* AL9....41 G1
Byde St *HERT/WAS* SG14....23 F1
Byfield *WGCW* AL8............9 E3

C

Calder Av *BRKMPK* AL9......42 D4
Calton Av *HERT/WAS* SG14....22 C1
Cameron Ct *WARE* SG12.....15 E3
Camfield *WGCE* AL7...........9 E1
Campfield Rd *HERT/WAS* SG14....23 E2
The Campus *WGCW* AL8......19 E1
Cannons Meadow *WLYN* AL6....10 D4
Canons Fld *WLYN* AL6.........4 B2
Canonsfield Rd *WLYN* AL6....4 B2
Canons Rd *WARE* SG12......14 D3
Caponfield *WGCE* AL7........20 A4
Cappell La *WARE* SG12......26 B3
Carde Cl *HERT/WAS* SG14....22 C1
Carleton Ri *WLYN* AL6........3 H4
Carve Ley *WGCE* AL7.........20 A3
Carvers Cft *KNEB* SG3........5 E1
Castle Ga *HERT/BAY* * SG13....23 F3
Castle Mead Gdns
HERT/WAS * SG14.............23 F2
Castle St *HERT/WAS* SG14....23 F2
Cautherly La *WARE* SG12....25 G3
Cavendish Wy *HAT* AL10.....34 D1
Caxton Hl *HERT/BAY* SG13....23 H2
Cecil Crs *HAT* AL10..........29 G4
Cecil Rd *HERT/BAY* SG13....23 F5
Cedar Cl *HERT/WAS* * SG14....23 E2
WGCE SG12.....................15 E5
Cedar Rd *HAT* AL10..........35 F2
Central Dr *WGCE* AL7..........9 G5
Century Rd *WARE* SG12......15 E3
Chadwell *WARE* SG12........14 D5
Chadwell Ri *WARE* SG12.....14 D5
Chain Wk *HERT/BAY* SG13....32 C5
HERT/BAY SG13................39 H4
HERT/WAS SG14................11 F3
HERT/WAS SG14................32 B1
WARE SG12.....................6 B1
Chalgrove *WGCE* AL7........20 C1
Chalk Dl *WGCE* AL7..........20 A1
Chambers' St *HERT/WAS* SG14....23 F2
Chandlers Wy *HERT/WAS* SG14....22 D2
Chantry La *HAT* AL10........35 E2
Chapelfields *WARE* SG12....26 C3
Chapel La *HERT/WAS* SG14....32 CJ
The Chase *HERT/BAY* SG13....24 A3
WARE SG12.....................25 H2
WLYN AL6.......................4 C3
Chauncy Cl *WARE* SG12......14 D2
Chedburgh *WGCE* AL7........20 C1
Chelmsford Rd *HERT/WAS* SG14....22 D3
Chelveston *WGCE* AL7........20 C1
Chelwood Av *HAT* AL10......29 F4
Chennells *HAT* AL10.........35 E2
Chequers *BRKMPK* AL9......30 A3
WGCE AL7......................19 E4
Chequers Fld *WGCE* AL7.....19 E5
Cherry Cft *WGCW* AL8........9 E3
Cherry Tree Gn *HERT/WAS* SG14....12 C5
Cherry Wy *HAT* AL10.........29 F4
Chestnut Av *WARE* SG12....15 G2
The Chestnuts *HERT/BAY* SG13....23 G3
Chestnut Wk *WLYN* AL6.......4 D2
Cheviots *HAT* AL10..........35 F4
Cheyne Cl *WARE* SG12......15 E2
Chiltern Cl *WARE* SG12.....15 E2
Chilterns *HAT* AL10.........35 H4
Chilton Gn *WGCE* AL7.......20 B2
Christopher Ct *WARE* * SG12....15 E4

Church Fld *WARE* SG12 ....14 C2
Churchfield Rd *WLYN* AL6.........10 B4
Churchfields *HERT/BAY* SG13.....23 G3
Church Hl *HERT/WAS* SG14 ....24 C4
Church La *BRKMPK* AL9.............35 H1
   STALE/WH AL4........................34 A5
Church Pl *WLYN* AL6..................3 E1
Church Rd *HERT/BAY* SG13........38 D2
   HERT/WAS SG14....................23 E1
   WGCW AL8.............................18 D2
Church St *BRKMPK* AL9.............29 H5
   BRKMPK AL9..........................31 H5
   HERT/WAS SG14....................23 G2
   WARE SG12.............................15 E4
   WLYN AL6................................3 H5
City Pk *WGCE* * AL7.................19 H1
Clarke's Rd *HAT* AL10..............29 G5
Clarks Cl *WARE* SG12................15 E2
Claycroft *WGCE* AL7..................20 A1
Clements St *WARE* SG12...........15 F4
Clifton Wy *WARE* SG12..............15 E2
The Cloisters *WGCW* AL8...........19 E2
The Close *BRKMPK* * AL9..........30 A5
   BRKMPK AL9..........................42 B4
   WARE SG12.............................15 F4
   WLYN AL6................................3 E1
Cloverfield *WGCE* AL7.................9 G4
Cloverland *HAT* AL10................35 E4
Clyde Ter *HERT/BAY* SG13.........24 B2
Coachhouse Ms
   HERT/WAS SG14....................23 F1
Cobham Rd *WARE* SG12............15 G3
Cob Lane Cl *WLYN* AL6...............9 G1
Cobmead *HAT* AL10..................29 G4
Cockbush Av *HERT/BAY* SG13....24 B1
Codicote Rd *WLYN* AL6...............3 F3
Cold Christmas La *WARE* SG12....7 G4
Cole Green La *WGCE* AL7............9 G4
Cole Green Wy *HERT/WAS* SG14..22 D4
Colgrove *WGCW* AL8.................18 D3
College Cl *WARE* SG12..............15 E5
College La *HAT* AL10.................34 D3
College Wy *WGCW* AL8.............19 E1
Collett Rd *WARE* SG12..............15 E3
The Colonnades *HAT* * AL10......29 H4
Coltsfoot *WGCE* AL7..................20 A4
Coltsfoot La *KNEB* SG3................5 C3
Coltsfoot Rd *WARE* SG12...........15 F2
Colyer Cl *WLYN* AL6....................9 C2
Comet Rd *HAT* AL10..................35 E1
Comet Wy *HAT* AL10.................29 F3
   HAT AL10..............................34 D1
The Commons *WGCE* AL7..........19 H5
The Common *HAT* AL10.............29 G5
Common Whf *WARE* SG12..........15 F4
Coney Cl *HAT* AL10...................35 G3
Coneydale *WGCW* AL8.................9 E5
Coningsby Cl *BRKMPK* AL9.........41 F1
Cooks Wy *HAT* AL10..................35 G3
Coopers Ct *WARE* * SG12...........15 F4
Coopers Green La *HAT* AL10.......28 B2
   WGCE AL7..............................29 E1
Copper Beeches *WLYN* AL6.........4 A3
Copperfields *WGCE* AL7.............20 B3
Copperwood *HERT/BAY* SG13.....24 A2
Coppice Cl *HAT* AL10.................35 E5
Copse Hl *WLYN* AL6....................4 D2
The Copse *HERT/BAY* SG13........24 B2
Corals Md *WGCE* AL7.................19 G4
Corncroft *HAT* AL10...................29 G4
Cornerfield *HAT* AL10.................29 G5
Corners *WGCE* AL7.....................19 H1
Corn Md *WGCW* AL8....................8 D4
Coronation Rd *WARE* SG12.........15 E3
Cotswolds *HAT* AL10..................35 F3
Cotton Dr *HERT/BAY* SG13.........24 C1
Cotton Fld *HAT* AL10.................29 G4
Coursers Rd *STALE/WH* AL4.......40 B3
Cowards La *WLYN* AL6.................3 E2
Cowbridge *HERT/WAS* SG14.......23 F2
Cowper Crs *HERT/WAS* SG14.....13 E4
Cowper Rd *WGCE* AL7................19 G4
Cowpers Wy *WLYN* AL6................5 C5
Cozens Rd *WARE* SG12..............15 G3
Cranborne Cl *HERT/BAY* SG13....23 F5
Cranborne Gdns *WGCE* AL7........19 G3
Cranborne Rd *HAT* AL10.............29 G5
Cranbrook Cl *WARE* SG12..........15 E2
Crane Md *WARE* SG12................15 F5
Crawford Rd *HAT* AL10..............29 F4
The Crescent *WLYN* AL6..............8 D1
Cresset St *WARE* SG12..............26 B5
The Crest *WARE* SG12...............15 E1
   WLYN AL6................................4 A2
Creswick Ct *WGCE* * AL7............19 E3
Crib St *WARE* SG12...................15 E3
Croft Fld *HAT* AL10....................35 E1
Croft Rd *WARE* SG12.................14 D3

The Croft *WARE* SG12................16 D1
   WGCE AL7.............................19 G5
Cromwell Rd *HERT/BAY* SG13....24 A1
   WARE SG12.............................15 G4
Crookhams *WGCE* AL7...............9 H5
Crop Common *HAT* AL10.............29 G4
Crossbrook *HAT* AL10................34 D2
Cross La *HERT/WAS* SG14.........23 E2
Cross Rd *HERT/WAS* SG14........23 F1
Cross St *WARE* SG12.................15 F4
Crossway *WGCW* AL8..................8 C3
Crouchfield *HERT/WAS* SG14......13 F4
Crouchfield La *WARE* SG12........13 H1
Cubitts Cl *WLYN* AL6...................9 G2
Cublands *HERT/BAY* SG13.........24 C2
Cucumber La *BRKMPK* AL9.........38 A4
Cumberland Cl *HERT/WAS* SG14..13 E4
Cundalls Rd *WARE* SG12...........15 F3
Currie St *HERT/BAY* SG13..........23 H1
Cutmore Dr *STALE/WH* AL4........34 A5
Cylers Thicket *WLYN* AL6.............3 H4
Cypress Av *WGCE* AL7...............20 B3

D

Dalewood *WGCE* AL7..................20 C3
Danesbury La *WLYN* AL6..............3 H2
Danesbury Pk *HERT/WAS* SG14...23 C1
   WLYN * AL6...............................3 H3
Danesbury Park Rd *WLYN* AL6......3 H3
Daniells *WGCE* AL7....................19 H1
Dark La *WLYN* AL6......................2 D2
Davies St *HERT/BAY* SG13.........23 H2
Dawley *WGCE* AL7......................20 A5
Dayemead *WGCE* AL7.................20 A5
Days Cl *HAT* AL10.......................35 E1
Days Md *HAT* AL10.....................35 E1
Deer Cl *HERT/BAY* SG13.............24 A2
Deerfield Cl *WARE* SG12.............15 E3
Deerswood Av *HAT* AL10............35 G3
De Havilland Cl *HAT* AL10...........29 E5
Delfcroft *WARE* SG12..................15 E2
Dellcott Cl *WGCW* AL8................18 C1
Dellfield *WARE* SG12....................7 E2
Dellfield Rd *HAT* AL10................35 F1
Dellsome La *STALE/WH* AL4........40 D1
Dellswood Cl *HERT/BAY* SG13.....23 H3
The Dell *HERT/BAY* SG13...........23 F5
Demontfort Ri *WARE* SG12..........14 D2
Densley Cl *HERT/WAS* SG14........8 D5
Desborough Rd *HERT/WAS* SG14..13 H4
Desborough Dr *WLYN* AL6...........5 F5
Dewars Cl *WLYN* AL6...................3 H4
Dicket Md *WLYN* AL6....................3 H5
Digswell La *WGCE* AL7.................9 G3
Digswell Park Rd *WGCW* AL8........9 F2
Digswell Ri *WGCW* AL8.................9 E5
Digswell Rd *WGCW* AL8................9 E5
Dimsdale St *HERT/WAS* SG14......23 F2
Divot Pl *HERT/BAY* SG13............24 C1
Dixons Ct *WARE* * SG12.............15 F5
Dixons Hill Cl *BRKMPK* AL9.........41 G3
Dixons Hill Rd *BRKMPK* AL9........41 G3
Dodwood *WGCE* AL7...................20 A3
Dog Kennel La *HAT* AL10............29 F5
Dognell Gn *WGCW* AL8...............18 C1
Dolesbury Dr *WLYN* AL6...............5 E1
Dolphin Yd *WARE* * SG12...........15 E4
Douglas Wy *WGCE* AL7...............20 B2
Dove Ct *HAT* AL10......................35 F3
Dovedale *WARE* SG12.................14 D2
Downfield Cl *HERT/BAY* SG13......24 A4
Downfield Ct *WARE* * SG12..........6 C5
Downfield Rd *HERT/BAY* SG13.....24 A4
Downfields *WGCW* AL8................18 C4
Downsfield *HAT* AL10..................35 F4
Downs La *HAT* AL10...................35 G4
The Downs *HAT* AL10.................35 G3
Drakes Wy *HAT* AL10.................35 G3
The Drive *BRKMPK* AL9...............42 D3
   HERT/WAS SG14....................13 F5
   WLYN AL6................................4 D1
Drovers Wy *WGCE* AL7...............20 A3
Drycroft *WGCE* AL7.....................30 B1
Ducketts Wd *WARE* SG12.............7 E3
Dudley Hill Cl *WLYN* AL6..............4 B2
Duncan Cl *WGCE* AL7.................19 F3
Duncombe Cl *HERT/WAS* SG14...13 F5
Duncombe Rd *HERT/WAS* SG14...23 F1
Dunsters Md *WGCE* AL7..............19 H4
Durham Cl *WGCE* AL7.................26 A3

E

Eagle Ct *HERT/BAY* SG13............24 C1
Eagle Wy *HAT* AL10....................35 F3
East Burrowfield *WGCE* AL7.........19 E4
East Md *WGCE* AL7....................20 A5
Eastor *WGCE* AL7........................9 H4
East Riding *WLYN* AL6.................5 C5
East St *WARE* SG12....................15 E4
East Vw *BRKMPK* AL9.................32 A5
Edgars Ct *WGCE* * AL7...............19 F3
Edmunds Rd *HERT/WAS* SG14....22 C1
Elder Rd *WARE* SG12..................15 G2
Eleanor Rd *HERT/WAS* SG14.......23 F1
Elizabeth Cl *WGCE* AL7...............20 B2
Ellenbrook Crs *HAT* AL10............34 C1
Ellenbrook La *HAT* AL10.............34 D2
Ellesfield *WLYN* AL6.....................3 C5
Elliott Cl *WGCE* AL7...................19 E5
Elm Dr *HAT* AL10........................35 F2
Elm Gdns *WGCW* AL8.................18 C2
Elmoor Av *WLYN* AL6....................3 C5
Elmoor Cl *WLYN* AL6....................8 C1
Elms Rd *WARE* SG12..................15 H3
The Elms *HERT/BAY* SG13..........24 B2
Elmwood *WGCW* AL8..................18 C3
Elton Rd *HERT/WAS* SG14..........23 F1
Ely Cl *HAT* AL10.........................29 E5
Emma's Crs *WARE* SG12.............26 A4
Endymion Ct *HAT* AL10...............29 H5
Endymion Ms *HAT* AL10..............29 H5
Endymion Rd *HAT* AL10..............29 H5
Ermine St *WARE* SG12..................7 E3
Essendon Gdns *WGCE* AL7.........19 G2
Essendon Hl *BRKMPK* AL9..........31 H5
Etheired Cl *WGCE* AL7................19 G3
Evergreen Rd *WARE* SG12...........15 G2
Extension Rd *HERT/BAY* SG13.....24 A2

F

Fairfax Rd *HERT/BAY* SG13.........24 A1
Fairway *WARE* SG12...................14 D5
Falcon Cl *HAT* AL10....................35 F3
Falcon Wy *WGCE* AL7.................35 F3
Fallow End *WLYN* AL6...................4 A1
Fallowfield *WGCE* AL7...................9 H2
Fallow Ri *HERT/BAY* SG13...........23 H2
Fanhams Gra *WARE* * SG12........15 H1
Fanhams Hall Rd *WARE* SG12......15 F2
Fanhams Rd *WARE* SG12............15 F2
Fanshaw Ct *HERT/WAS* SG14......23 E1
Fanshawe Crs *WARE* SG12..........14 C3
Fanshawe St *HERT/WAS* SG14....23 E1
Far End *HAT* AL10.......................35 G4
Farm Cl *HERT/WAS* SG14...........22 D2
   WGCW AL8.............................18 D2
Farquhar St *HERT/WAS* SG14......23 F1
Farriers *WARE* SG12...................25 H2
Farriers Cl *WLYN* AL6...................3 E1
Farriers Ct *WARE* SG12..............25 H2
Fawn Ct *BRKMPK* AL9................29 H4
Fearnley Rd *WGCW* AL8..............18 D3
Feather Dell *HAT* AL10................35 E1
Fellowes La *STALE/WH* AL4.........40 C1
Fern Dells *HAT* AL10...................35 E2
Fern Gv *WGCW* AL8.....................9 E3
Fiddle Bridge La *HAT* AL10..........29 E5
Fieldway *WGCE* SG12.................26 A4
Finch Cl *HAT* AL10......................35 F3
The Finches *HERT/BAY* SG13......24 C2
Firbank *WGCW* * AL8..................18 D2
Firs Cl *HAT* AL10........................35 G2
The Firs Pk *BRKMPK* * AL9.........42 D1
The Firs *WGCW* AL8.....................8 D3
Firs Wk *WLYN* AL6.......................5 C5
Firway *WLYN* AL6.........................4 C3
Firway Cl *WLYN* AL6.....................4 C3
Five Oaks *HAT* * AL10.................35 G4
Fleming Crs *HERT/WAS* SG14......22 C2
Flexley Wd *WGCE* AL7..................9 G4
The Folly *HERT/WAS* SG14..........23 G2
Folly Vw *WARE* SG12..................26 A3
Fordwich Cl *HERT/WAS* SG14......22 D2
Fordwich Hl *HERT/WAS* SG14......22 D2
Fordwich Ri *HERT/WAS* SG14......22 D2
Fordwich Rd *WGCW* AL8.............18 D3
Fore St *BRKMPK* AL9..................29 H5
   HERT/WAS SG14....................23 G2
Forge La *WLYN* AL6......................3 G5
Forresters Dr *WGCE* AL7.............20 B3
Forum Pl *HAT* * AL10..................29 F5
Fountain Dr *HERT/BAY* SG13.......24 A1
Four Acres *WGCE* AL7.................19 F4
Foxdells *HERT/WAS* SG14............21 H5

Foxes Cl *HERT/BAY* SG13...........24 C2
Foxglove Cl *HAT* AL10................35 G2
Foxglove Wy *WLYN* AL6................4 B2
Foxholes Av *HERT/BAY* SG13......24 B2
Foxley Gv *WLYN* AL6....................9 F1
Foxhollows *HAT* AL10.................29 G4
Fox's La *BRKMPK* AL9................42 B2
Frampton St *HERT/WAS* SG14.....23 G2
Francis Rd *WARE* SG12...............15 E3
Franklin Cl *STALE/WH* AL4...........34 D5
French Horn Ct *WARE* * SG12.....15 E4
French Horn La *HAT* AL10...........29 G5
French's Cl *WARE* SG12..............25 H1
Fretherne Chambers
   WGCW * AL8............................19 E2
Fretherne Rd *WGCW* AL8............19 E2
Frobisher Wy *HAT* AL10..............28 C3
Frowick Cl *BRKMPK* AL9.............41 G4
Fulling Mill La *WLYN* AL6..............3 G4
Furlong Wy *WARE* SG12.............25 G2
Furzefield Rd *WGCE* AL7............19 F1
Furzen Crs *HAT* AL10.................35 E5

G

Gaddesden Gv *WGCE* AL7...........20 A4
Gainswood *WGCE* AL7................19 F4
The Galleria *HAT* * AL10.............29 E5
Garden Av *HAT* AL10..................35 F4
The Gardens *BRKMPK* AL9..........42 B4
Garden Ter *WARE* * SG12...........13 H4
Garland Rd *WARE* SG12..............15 F4
Gascoyne Wy *HERT/BAY* SG13....23 G2
Gentlemens Fld *WARE* SG12........14 C4
George St *HERT/WAS* SG14.........23 F1
George's Wood Rd *BRKMPK* AL9..42 B2
George Wk *WARE* SG12...............15 E4
Gilpin Rd *WARE* SG12.................15 G2
Gilpin's Gallop *WARE* SG12..........26 A5
The Glade *WGCW* AL8..................8 C2
Gladstone Rd *WARE* SG12..........14 D4
Glebe Cl *BRKMPK* AL9................32 A5
   HERT/WAS SG14....................13 F4
Glebe Cottages *BRKMPK* AL9......32 A5
Glebe Rd *HERT/WAS* SG14..........13 F4
   WLYN AL6................................3 E1
Glenfield Ct *HERT/WAS* SG14......22 C1
Glenwood *WGCE* AL7..................20 A4
Glovers Cl *HERT/BAY* SG13.........23 H2
Goblins Gn *WGCE* AL7................19 F4
Goddards Cl *HERT/BAY* SG13......38 D2
Godfries Cl *WLYN* AL6................10 B4
Golden Dell *HAT* AL10.................30 C1
Goldings Crs *HAT* AL10...............29 F5
Goldings La *HERT/WAS* SG14......12 D4
Goldstone Cl *WARE* SG12...........15 F3
Golf Club Rd *BRKMPK* AL9..........42 D1
Gomer Cl *HITCHE/RSTV* SG4........2 A1
Gooseacre *WGCE* AL7................19 F4
Gorse Cl *HAT* AL10.....................35 F3
Gosselin Rd *HERT/WAS* SG14......13 F4
Gould Cl *BRKMPK* AL9...............41 F1
The Granary *WARE* SG12.............26 A5
Grange Cl *HERT/WAS* SG14.........23 F2
Grange Ct *HERT/WAS* * SG14......23 F2
Grange Gdns *WARE* SG12...........15 G3
Grange Hl *WLYN* AL6....................3 H5
Grange Ri *WLYN* AL6....................3 H5
The Grange *STALE/WH* * AL4.......40 C1
Grantham Gdns *WARE* SG12........15 G3
Grasmere Rd *WARE* SG12...........15 E1
Grass Warren *WLYN* AL6.............10 A3
Graveley Dell *WGCE* AL7.............19 G4
Graysfield *WGCE* AL7..................19 G4
Great Braitch La *HAT* AL10..........28 A4
Great Break *WGCE* AL7...............20 A4
Great Conduit *WGCE* AL7............20 A4
Great Dell *WGCW* AL8..................8 D2
Great Ganett *WGCE* AL7.............20 A5
Great Heath *HAT* AL10................29 E4
Great Ley *WGCE* AL7..................19 H5
Great Molewood
   HERT/WAS SG14....................13 G1
Great North Rd *BRKMPK* AL9.......31 H5
   BRKMPK AL9..........................41 H1
   WGCW AL8.............................18 C4
   WGCW AL8.............................28 C1
   WLYN AL6..............................18 C1
Green Acres *WGCE* * AL7............19 H1
Green Cl *BRKMPK* AL9................32 A5
Greencoates *HERT/BAY* SG13......23 G2
Green Cft *HAT* AL10....................29 H5
Green End *WLYN* AL6....................9 G1
Greenfield *BRKMPK* AL9.............32 A5
   WGCW AL8.............................18 C3
Greenhills *WARE* SG12...............15 E4

La WGCE AL7 ...20 B4
AL10 ...29 E3
CW AL8 ...18 A4
een WARE SG12 ...15 E2
n AL6 ...2 D1
AL6 ...3 C5
V WGCE AL7 ...19 H3
ways HERT/WAS SG14 ...23 E2
AL6 ...9 F2
Cl WGCW AL8 ...19 F1
e Cl BRKMPK AL9 ...41 G2
riars WARE SG12 ...14 C2
otto WARE SG12 ...15 E5
d HAT AL10 ...29 G4
Lea HAT AL10 ...35 F4
Md HAT AL10 ...35 E1
Meadow WCCE AL7 ...20 B2
Pl BRKMPK AL9 ...41 H2
Rd WARE SG12 ...15 G3
ove BRKMPK AL9 ...42 D5
ns La HERT/WAS SG14 ...13 F5
s La WCCE AL7 ...36 D5
ens Gv WCCW AL8 ...18 D2
ens Rd WCCW AL8 ...18 D2
ek Wk WCCW AL8 ...18 D1
ulphs HERT/BAY SG13 ...23 G3
fa Cl WLYN AL6 ...4 A3
ns Wk HERT/BAY SG13 ...23 H2
Cl WARE SG12 ...25 G4
La BRKMPK AL9 ...30 C2
RE SG12 ...25 G4

H

dell Rd HERT/BAY SG13 ...23 G3
ns WGCE AL7 ...9 G4
Rd HERT/BAY SG13 ...23 G3
x Wy WGCE AL7 ...20 D2
rs Rdg HERT/WAS SG14 ...22 D3
ns STALE/WH AL4 ...40 C1
v WGCE AL7 ...20 A4
Cl WLYN AL6 ...8 D1
de HAT AL10 ...34 C2
ls Dr HERT/BAY SG13 ...24 C1
ton Ct HAT * AL10 ...35 G3
den HI WARE SG12 ...15 G4
den Hill Cl WARE SG12 ...15 G4
ury Cl WARE SG12 ...15 E4
ury Ct WARE SG12 ...6 D4
ury Ms WARE * SG12 ...6 D5
side HI WCCE AL7 ...18 D2
side Gn WCCW AL8 ...18 D1
mans La WLYN AL6 ...4 C2
ver Wk HAT AL10 ...35 E4
mlow Wy WARE SG12 ...17 F5
ngs WGCE AL7 ...20 B1
ell WCCE AL7 ...30 B1
ell Cl HERT/BAY SG13 ...24 C2
La HAT AL10 ...35 G3
rde Ct HERT/BAY * SG13 ...24 B2
er Dell WLYN AL6 ...9 G1
er Green La WLYN AL6 ...9 G1
ony Cl HAT AL10 ...35 F2
sfield Broadway HAT AL10 ...29 E5
s's La WARE SG12 ...14 D4
am Common
PT/WAS * SG14 ...23 G1
am La HERT/BAY SG13 ...23 F2
AL6 ...4 B3
st WARE SG12 ...15 E2
st Md HAT AL10 ...29 C5
ood Cl WCCW AL8 ...18 D3
N AL6 ...10 D3
ood HI WCCW AL8 ...9 F4
dine Mdw HAT AL10 ...35 E2
eld Av HAT AL10 ...29 E3
eld Rd BRKMPK AL9 ...30 D2
LE/WH AL4 ...34 B2
La HAT AL10 ...29 E5
azels WLYN * AL6 ...10 D3
brow Rd WLYN AL6 ...4 B2
cote Av HAT AL10 ...29 F4
croft WCCE AL7 ...20 B1
r Dr WARE SG12 ...15 E2
CE AL7 ...20 A1
er Rd WGCW AL8 ...18 D4

Heathgate HERT/BAY SG13 ...24 C5
Heath HI HTCHE/RSTV SG4 ...2 C1
Heathlands WLYN AL6 ...4 C1
Heath La HTCHE/RSTV SG4 ...2 D1
Heath Rd WLYN AL6 ...4 C1
Heathside STALE/WH AL4 ...40 A1
Heay Flds WGCE AL7 ...20 B1
Hedgebrooms WGCE AL7 ...20 B1
Hedges Cl HAT AL10 ...29 C5
Hempstall WGCE AL7 ...20 A4
Hensley Cl WLYN AL6 ...3 H4
Herneshaw HAT AL10 ...35 E3
Herns La WCCE AL7 ...20 A2
Herns Wy WGCE AL7 ...9 H5
Heron Dr WARE SG12 ...26 B5
Heronswood Pl WGCE AL7 ...19 H3
Heronswood Rd WGCE AL7 ...19 C2
Heron Wy HAT AL10 ...35 F3
Hertford Rd BRKMPK AL9 ...30 A4
BRKMPK AL9 ...31 G2
WARE SG12 ...15 E5
WARE SG12 ...25 G4
WLYN AL6 ...3 H5
WLYN AL6 ...11 G1
Hertfordshire Wy
HERT/WAS SG14 ...12 D3
Hertingfordbury Rd
HERT/WAS SG14 ...22 B4
Heybridge Ct HERT/WAS SG14 ...22 C1
Heyford Wy HAT AL10 ...29 H4
High Dells HAT AL10 ...35 E2
Highfield Rd HERT/BAY SG13 ...23 G4
Highlands BRKMPK AL9 ...29 H3
High Oak Rd WARE SG12 ...15 E3
High Oaks Rd WCCW AL8 ...18 C1
High Rd BRKMPK AL9 ...37 H1
HERT/WAS SG14 ...12 D2
High St STALE/WH AL4 ...34 B5
WARE SG12 ...15 E4
WARE SG12 ...26 B4
WLYN AL6 ...3 E1
WLYN AL6 ...3 H5
High Vw HAT AL10 ...35 E3
High Wickfield WGCE AL7 ...20 B3
Hilbury Rd HAT AL10 ...35 E2
Hillcrest HAT AL10 ...35 F2
Hill Farm La WLYN AL6 ...2 B5
Hillfield HAT AL10 ...29 G3
Hill Ley HAT AL10 ...35 E1
Hill Rd HTCHE/RSTV SG4 ...2 D1
Hillside HAT AL10 ...35 F1
WARE SG12 ...15 E5
WCCE AL7 ...20 A5
AL6 ...3 C1
Hillside Crs WARE SG12 ...26 A4
Hillside La WARE SG12 ...25 H3
Hillside Ter HERT/BAY SG13 ...23 F4
Hillside Wy WLYN AL6 ...4 D2
Hilly Flds WCCE AL7 ...20 B1
Hitches Yd WARE * SG12 ...15 E4
Hitherbaulk WCCE AL7 ...19 E4
Hither Fld WARE SG12 ...15 F2
Hitherway WGCW AL8 ...18 D3
Hobbs Wy WCCW AL8 ...18 D3
Hocklands WGCE AL7 ...20 B1
Hoddesdon Rd WARE SG12 ...26 B4
Hoe La WARE SG12 ...25 E2
Hogsdell La HERT/BAY SG13 ...24 C4
Holden Cl HERT/BAY SG13 ...23 H1
The Holdings BRKMPK AL9 ...30 A4
Holliers Wy HAT AL10 ...35 F1
Holloways La BRKMPK AL9 ...42 A1
Hollybush Cl WLYN AL6 ...4 B2
Hollybush La BRKMPK AL9 ...30 C1
WCCE AL7 ...19 F5
Holly Cl HAT AL10 ...35 E2
Holly Cft HERT/WAS SG14 ...22 C1
Hollycross Rd WARE SG12 ...15 G5
Holly Dell HERT/BAY SG13 ...23 F4
Hollyfield HAT AL10 ...35 F4
Holly Grove Rd HERT/WAS SG14 ...11 H2
Holly Hall Ct WLYN AL6 ...3 H5
Holly Rd KNEB SG3 ...4 D1
Holly Wk HAT AL10 ...8 D3
Holme Cl HAT AL10 ...29 G3
Holme Rd HAT AL10 ...29 G3
The Holt WGCE AL7 ...20 C5
Holwell Hyde WGCE AL7 ...20 B4
Holwell Hyde La BRKMPK AL9 ...31 F1
Holwell La BRKMPK AL9 ...31 H2
Holwell Rd WGCE AL7 ...19 F3
Homefield Rd WARE SG12 ...15 F3
Home Ley WGCE AL7 ...19 F2
Home Meadow WGCE AL7 ...19 F2
Homefield WGCE AL7 ...18 D2
Homerswood La WLYN AL6 ...8 B3
Homestead La WGCE AL7 ...19 G5

Homestead Rd HAT AL10 ...29 F3
Honeycroft WGCW AL8 ...18 D3
Honeysuckle Cl HERT/BAY SG13 ...24 B2
Honeysuckle Gdns HAT AL10 ...35 G2
Hornbeam La BRKMPK AL9 ...37 H4
Hornbeams WGCE * AL7 ...20 A3
Horns Cl HERT/BAY SG13 ...23 E5
Hornsfield WGCE AL7 ...20 B1
Horns Mill Rd HERT/BAY SG13 ...23 E5
Horns Rd HERT/BAY SG13 ...23 E5
Horrocks Cl WARE SG12 ...15 E2
Howardsgate WGCW AL8 ...19 E3
Howe Dell HAT AL10 ...35 G1
Howicks Gn WGCE AL7 ...19 H5
Howlands WGCE AL7 ...19 F5
Huggins La BRKMPK AL9 ...41 H1
Hunsdon WGCE AL7 ...20 C2
Hunsdon Rd WARE SG12 ...26 D4
Hunters Wy WGCE AL7 ...19 G5
Hurst Cl WGCE AL7 ...20 B3
Hurstlings WGCE AL7 ...20 A4
Hutton Cl HERT/WAS SG14 ...22 D2
The Hyde WARE SG12 ...14 C3
Hyde Va WGCE AL7 ...19 G4
Hyde Wy WGCE AL7 ...19 F2

I

Indells HAT AL10 ...35 E2
Ingles WGCW AL8 ...9 F4
Iron Dr HERT/BAY SG13 ...24 C1
Ives Rd HERT/WAS SG14 ...23 E1

J

Jackdaws WGCE AL7 ...20 B2
Jasmine Dr HERT/BAY SG13 ...24 B2
Jasmine Gdns HAT AL10 ...29 E4
Jenning Wd WLYN AL6 ...4 C3
The Jinnings WGCE AL7 ...20 A4
John Tate Rd HERT/BAY SG13 ...24 A3
Jonquil Cl WGCE AL7 ...20 A4
Jubilee Av WARE SG12 ...15 G3

K

Katescroft WGCE AL7 ...30 B1
Kelbys WGCE AL7 ...20 B1
Kendall Cl WGCE AL7 ...30 C1
Kennelwood La HAT AL10 ...29 G5
Kentish La BRKMPK AL9 ...43 F2
Kestrel Gn HAT AL10 ...35 F3
Kestrel Wy WGCE AL7 ...20 C5
Keynton Cl HERT/WAS SG14 ...22 C1
Kibes La WARE SG12 ...15 E4
Kilnfield WGCE AL7 ...19 H2
Kiln House Ct WARE SG12 ...15 F3
Kilworth Cl WGCE AL7 ...20 A4
Kimpton Rd HTCHE/RSTV SG4 ...2 B1
WLYN AL6 ...2 D4
Kindersley Cl WLYN AL6 ...3 H4
King Edward's Rd WARE SG12 ...15 F4
Kingfisher Cl WGCE AL7 ...19 H5
King George Rd WARE SG12 ...15 F3
Kingscroft WGCE AL7 ...20 A1
Kingsley Ct BRKMPK AL9 ...30 C1
Kingsmill Ct HAT AL10 ...35 G3
King's Rd HERT/BAY SG13 ...24 B1
Kingsway WARE SG12 ...15 E2
Kirklands WGCE AL7 ...19 H3
Knella Gn WGCE AL7 ...19 H2
Knella Rd WGCE AL7 ...19 H2
Knightsfield WGCW AL8 ...9 E3
Knolles Crs BRKMPK AL9 ...41 G2
The Knoll HERT/BAY SG13 ...24 C1

L

Lady Gv WGCE AL7 ...30 B1
Lady St John Sq
HERT/WAS * SG14 ...22 D2
Ladywood Rd HERT/WAS SG14 ...22 C2
Lamb Cl HAT AL10 ...35 G2
Lane End HAT AL10 ...35 E4
Lanefield Wk WCCW AL8 ...18 D2
Lanercost Cl WLYN AL6 ...4 C3
The Larches WARE SG12 ...15 G4
Lark Ri HAT AL10 ...35 F3
Larksfield WARE SG12 ...15 F2
Latimer Gdns WGCE AL7 ...20 A2

The Lawns WGCW AL8 ...9 E4
Lawrence Av WARE SG12 ...26 B4
Lawrence Cl HERT/WAS SG14 ...22 B1
Lea Gn BRKMPK * AL9 ...30 B3
Lea Valley Wk BRKMPK AL9 ...29 H1
BRKMPK AL9 ...32 A2
HERT/BAY SG13 ...23 H1
HERT/WAS SG14 ...21 H5
WARE SG12 ...25 H4
WCCW AL8 ...18 A2
Lee Cl HERT/BAY SG13 ...23 F4
WARE SG12 ...26 B4
Leigh Common WGCE AL7 ...19 F4
Lemsford La WGCW AL8 ...18 C3
Lemsford Rd HAT AL10 ...29 E5
Lemsford Village WGCW AL8 ...18 A3
Leonard's Cl WLYN AL6 ...4 B2
Leysdown WGCE AL7 ...20 C2
Ley Wk WGCE AL7 ...20 B2
Liberty Cl HERT/BAY SG13 ...23 F4
The Limberlost WLYN AL6 ...3 C3
Lime Cl WARE SG12 ...15 F3
The Limes WGCE AL7 ...19 H4
Linces Wy WGCE AL7 ...19 F4
Lincoln Cl WGCE AL7 ...20 B1
Lindbergh WGCE AL7 ...20 B1
The Lindens HAT * AL10 ...29 E5
Link Cl HAT AL10 ...35 G1
Link Dr HAT AL10 ...35 G1
Linkfield WGCE AL7 ...30 B1
Link Rd WLYN AL6 ...4 C3
Links Av HERT/BAY SG13 ...24 C1
Linwood Rd WARE SG12 ...15 G2
Little Acres WARE SG12 ...15 E5
Little Berkhamstead La
BRKMPK AL9 ...38 A3
Little Burrow WGCE AL7 ...19 E4
Little Dell WGCW AL8 ...9 E5
Little Ganett WGCE AL7 ...20 A4
Little Hardings WGCE AL7 ...20 B1
Little Lake WGCE AL7 ...20 A5
Little Ley WGCE AL7 ...19 F5
Little Md HAT AL10 ...29 C5
Little Mundells WGCE AL7 ...19 G1
Little Rdg WGCE AL7 ...19 H2
Little Rivers WGCE AL7 ...19 H1
Little Thistle WGCE AL7 ...20 B4
Little Wade WGCE AL7 ...19 G5
Little Widbury WARE SG12 ...15 G4
Little Widbury La WARE SG12 ...15 G4
Little Youngs WGCW AL8 ...18 D2
Lockley Crs HAT AL10 ...29 G4
Lockleys Dr WLYN AL6 ...3 H5
Lodge Cl HERT/WAS SG14 ...13 G5
Lodge Dr BRKMPK AL9 ...30 A3
Lodge Fld WGCE AL7 ...9 F4
London Rd HERT/BAY SG13 ...24 A3
WARE SG12 ...15 G5
WLYN AL6 ...3 G1
Longcroft Gdns WGCW AL8 ...19 E3
Longcroft Gn WCCW AL8 ...19 E3
Longcroft La WGCW AL8 ...19 E3
Longlands Rd WGCE AL7 ...19 G4
Long Ley WGCE AL7 ...20 B2
Longmead HAT AL10 ...29 G3
Longmore Gdns WGCE AL7 ...19 G2
Longwood Rd HERT/WAS SG14 ...22 C1
Lord Mead La WLYN AL6 ...2 B3
Lords Wd WGCE AL7 ...20 B2
Lower Bourne Gdns WARE SG12 ...14 D2
Lower Clabdens WARE SG12 ...15 G4
Lowerfield WGCE AL7 ...19 H3
Lower Hatfield Rd
HERT/BAY SG13 ...33 F3
Lower Mardley HI WLYN AL6 ...4 C2
Lower Rd WARE SG12 ...25 G2
Lowlands BRKMPK AL9 ...29 H3
Low Rd BRKMPK AL9 ...32 A3
Loxley Ct WARE * SG12 ...15 F4
Ludwick Cl WGCE * AL7 ...19 G4
Ludwick Gn WGCE * AL7 ...19 G4
Ludwick Wy WGCE AL7 ...19 G4
Lumbards WGCE AL7 ...9 H4
Lydia Ms BRKMPK AL9 ...41 H2
Lygean Av WARE SG12 ...15 F4
Lyles La WCCW AL8 ...9 F5
Lynmouth Rd WGCE AL7 ...19 G2
Lysander Wy WGCE AL7 ...20 C1
Lys Hill Gdns HERT/WAS SG14 ...13 E5
Lytton Gdns WGCW AL8 ...19 E2

M

Madgeways Cl WARE * SG12 ...25 G3
Madgeways La WARE SG12 ...25 G3
Magnolia Cl HERT/BAY SG13 ...24 B2

Maidenhead St HERT/WAS SG14 ....23 G2
Maidenhead Yd
HERT/WAS SG14 ....23 G2
Main Rd HERT/WAS SG14 ......11 H2
Malmsdale WGCW AL8 ....9 E3
The Malthouse
HERT/WAS * SG14 ....23 G2
Malting Md HAT * AL10 ....29 H5
Malting Ms HERT/BAY * SG13 ....23 F5
The Maltings HERT/BAY * SG13 ....23 F5
Mandeville Cl HERT/BAY SG13 ...23 F5
Mandeville Ri WGCW AL8 ....9 E5
Mandeville Rd HERT/BAY SG13 ...23 F5
Mangrove Dr HERT/BAY SG13 ...23 H4
Mangrove La HERT/BAY SG13 ...23 H5
Mangrove Rd HERT/BAY SG13 ...23 H5
Mannicotts WGCW AL8 ....18 C2
Manor Cl HAT AL10...............29 E3
HERT/WAS SG14 ....13 C5
Manor Pde HAT AL10..............29 E3
Manor Rd HAT AL10..............29 E3
Mansfield Gdns HERT/WAS SG14...13 F5
Maple Cl HAT AL10 ....35 F2
Maple Gv WGCW AL7..............9 G4
Maplewood WARE SG12 ....14 D2
Maran Av WLYN AL6 ....8 D1
Mardlebury Rd KNEB SG3..........4 D1
Mardley Av WLYN AL6..........4 C2
Mardleybury Rd KNEB SG3..........4 D1
Mardley Dell WLYN AL6..........4 C1
Mardley Hts WLYN AL6..........4 C2
Mardley Hl WLYN AL6..........4 C1
Mardley Wd WLYN AL6..........4 C1
Marford Rd WGCW AL8..........18 A3
Margery Wd WGCE AL7..........9 H3
Market Pl HAT AL10..............29 G5
HERT/WAS * SG14 ....23 G2
Market St HERT/WAS SG14 ......23 G2
Marlborough Cl WLYN AL6..........4 C2
Marley Rd WGCE AL7..........19 H4
Marsden Cl WGCW AL8 ....18 C4
Marsden Gn WGCW AL8 ....18 C3
Marsden Rd WGCW AL8 ....18 C3
Marshgate Dr HERT/BAY SG13...23 H1
Marsh La WARE SG12..........15 F5
WARE SG12..........26 C5
Marshmoor Crs BRKMPK AL9..........36 A5
Marshmoor La BRKMPK AL9 ....35 H5
Martin Cl HAT AL10..............35 F1
Martinfield WGCE AL7..........19 C1
Martins Dr HERT/BAY SG13 ......24 C2
Maryland HAT AL10..............35 E1
Mary Proud Ct WLYN * AL6..........4 B3
Mayfield WGCW AL8..........8 D3
Mayflower Cl HERT/WAS SG14...22 B4
WLYN AL6..........3 E1
McDonald Ct HAT AL10..........35 F3
Mead La HERT/BAY SG13 ......23 H1
Meadow Cl BRKMPK AL9 ....42 D2
HERT/BAY SG13..........24 A1
Meadow Cft HAT AL10..........35 E1
Meadow Dell HAT AL10..........35 E1
Meadow Gn WGCW AL8..........18 D2
The Meadow WGCE AL7..........20 B2
Meadow Wy HTCHE/RSTV SG4..........2 D1
Meadview Rd WARE SG12 ....14 D5
Meadway STALE/WH AL4 ....40 C1
WGCE AL7..........19 G4
Melbourne Ct WGCW AL8..........18 C3
Mendlesham WGCE AL7..........20 D2
Merchant Dr HERT/BAY SG13......24 A1
Meridian Wy WARE SG12..........26 A3
Merritt Wk BRKMPK AL9..........41 G2
Middlefield HAT AL10..........29 F5
WGCE AL7..........30 B1
Millacres WARE * SG12..........15 F4
Mill Br HERT/WAS SG14 ......23 F2
Mill Cl WARE SG12..........15 E4
WGCW AL8..........18 B3
Millers La WARE SG12..........26 B4
Millers Yd HERT/WAS SG14 ......23 G2
Millfield WARE SG12..........7 F2
WGCE AL7..........20 B1
Mill Green La BRKMPK AL9..........30 B2
Mill Green Rd WGCE AL7..........19 F3
Mill La WLYN AL6..........3 H5
Millmead Wy HERT/WAS SG14...23 E1
Mill Race WGCE AL7..........26 C4
Mill Rd HERT/BAY SG13 ......23 G1
Millstream Cl HERT/WAS * SG14...23 E2
Millwards HAT AL10..........35 G4
Milton Rd WARE SG12..........15 E3
Mimram Rd HERT/WAS SG14 ......23 E3
WLYN AL6..........3 H5
The Minims HAT AL10..........29 H5
Minster Cl HAT AL10..........35 F3
Mitchell Cl WGCE AL7..........20 B2

Mitre Ct HERT/WAS * SG14..........23 G2
Moatwood Gn WGCE AL7..........19 F3
Moffats Cl HERT/WAS * SG14..........42 D4
Moffats La BRKMPK AL9..........42 B5
Molewood Rd HERT/WAS SG14..........23 E1
Money Hole La WLYN AL6..........20 D1
Monks Ri WGCW AL8..........9 E3
Monks Rw WARE SG12..........15 E3
Monkswood WGCW AL8..........8 D3
Moorend WGCE AL7..........19 H5
Moorlands WGCE AL7..........19 H5
Moorside WGCE AL7..........19 H5
The Moors WGCE AL7..........19 H1
Moors Wk WGCE AL7..........20 A1
Morgans Cl HERT/BAY SG13..........23 G4
Morgan's Rd HERT/BAY SG13..........23 G4
Morgan's Wk HERT/BAY SG13..........23 G5
Mornington WLYN AL6..........9 H1
Morrell Ct WGCE * AL7..........19 G1
Moss Gn WGCE AL7..........19 F4
Mount Pleasant Cl BRKMPK AL9...29 H3
Mount Pleasant La
BRKMPK AL9..........29 H3
Mount Rd HERT/WAS SG14..........22 D3
Mountsorrel HERT/BAY SG13..........24 A2
Mount Wy WGCE AL7..........19 G5
Mountway Cl WGCE AL7..........19 G5
Mundells WGCE AL7..........19 G1
Musleigh Mnr WARE SG12..........15 G4
Musley Hl WARE SG12..........15 F3
Musley La WARE SG12..........15 F3
Myddleton Rd WARE SG12..........15 E5
Mymms Dr BRKMPK AL9..........42 D5

N

Nash Cl BRKMPK AL9..........42 A1
Nathans Cl WLYN AL6..........3 H3
Neal Ct HERT/WAS SG14..........23 F2
Nelson St HERT/WAS SG14..........23 E1
Netherfield La WARE SG12..........26 D5
Nettlecroft WGCE AL7..........20 A1
The New Ar HERT/WAS * SG14..........23 G2
Newfields WGCW AL8..........18 C3
New Pl WLYN AL6..........8 C1
New River Av WARE SG12..........26 A4
New Rd HERT/WAS SG14..........15 C5
WARE SG12..........15 F4
WGCW AL8..........18 B5
WLYN AL6..........9 G2
Newstead HAT AL10..........35 E4
New Town WLYN AL6..........3 E1
New Wd WGCE AL7..........20 B1
Nicholas La HERT/WAS SG14..........23 G2
The Nook WARE SG12..........26 A4
Norman Rd WLYN AL6..........8 C2
Northdown Rd HAT AL10..........35 F4
North Dr STDN..........7 C1
North Orbital Rd STALE/WH AL4..........34 B4
North Ride WLYN AL6..........3 H4
North Rd HERT/WAS SG14..........23 F2
North Road Av HERT/WAS SG14 ...22 D3
North Road Gdns
HERT/WAS SG14..........23 E2
Northway WGCE AL7..........9 G4
Northwood WGCE AL7..........20 C2
Norwood Cl HERT/WAS SG14..........22 C1
Nursery Gdns WGCE AL7..........9 F4
Nursery Hl WGCE AL7..........9 F4
Nutfield WGCE AL7..........9 H4
Nut Gv WGCW AL8..........9 E4

O

Oakdale WGCW AL8..........9 E4
Oaken Gv WGCE AL7..........19 F5
Oak Gv HAT AL10..........35 E1
HERT/BAY SG13..........23 H4
Oakhill Dr WLYN AL6..........3 H4
Oakington WGCE AL7..........20 C2
Oaklands Av BRKMPK AL9..........42 B5
Oaklands Ri WLYN AL6..........4 B3
Oaklea WLYN AL6..........4 B3
Oaklea Cl WLYN AL6..........4 B3
Oaklea Wd WLYN AL6..........4 B3
Oak Piece WLYN AL6..........4 A3
Oak Rd KNEB SG3..........5 E1
Oak Tree Cl HAT AL10..........29 F5
HERT/BAY SG13..........24 D5
Oak Tree Ct WLYN * AL6..........4 B2
Oaktree Garth WGCE AL7..........19 F3
Old Church La WARE SG12..........7 F3
The Old Coach Rd
HERT/WAS SG14..........21 E5

Old Cross HERT/WAS * SG14..........23 F2
HERT/WAS SG14..........23 F2
The Old Dr WGCW AL8..........18 C3
Old Forge Cl WGCE AL7..........9 C3
Old Forge Rw HERT/BAY * SG13 ...24 C5
Old French Horn La HAT AL10 ...29 C5
Oldhall St HERT/WAS SG14..........23 G2
Old Herns La WGCE AL7..........10 B5
Old Hertford Rd BRKMPK AL9...29 H4
Oldings Cnr HAT AL10..........29 G2
Old Leys HAT AL10..........35 F5
Old London Rd HERT/BAY SG13...23 H2
The Old Maltings
HERT/BAY * SG13..........23 F3
Old Rectory Dr HAT AL10..........35 G1
Old School La HTCHE/RSTV SG4..........3 E1
Oldwood WLYN AL6..........4 B3
Oliver Ct WGCW AL8..........18 C3
Omega Ct WARE * SG12..........13 H1
Omega Maltings WARE * SG12...15 F4
Onslow Cl HAT AL10..........35 G1
The Opening WLYN AL6..........3 E2
Orchard Cl WARE SG12..........15 E3
WARE SG12..........26 B4
Orchard Md HAT AL10..........35 E1
Orchard Rd WLYN AL6..........3 H5
WLYN AL6..........5 F5
The Orchard HERT/WAS SG14...13 E4
WGCW AL8..........9 F5
WLYN AL6..........2 D1
Osborn Wy WGCW AL8..........19 E1
Otter Gdns HAT AL10..........35 G1
Ottway Wk WLYN AL6..........8 C1
Oxlease Dr HAT AL10..........35 G2

P

The Paddocks HERT/BAY SG13 ...24 C5
STALE/WH * AL4..........34 A5
WGCE AL7..........20 A1
WLYN AL6..........3 E1
The Paddock HAT AL10..........29 F5
Page Hl WARE SG12..........14 C3
Page Rd HERT/BAY SG13..........24 B2
Palmer Cl HERT/WAS SG14..........13 F5
Palmer Rd HERT/WAS SG14..........13 G5
Palmerston Cl WGCW AL8..........18 D2
Panshanger Dr WGCE AL7..........20 A2
The Parade HAT * AL10..........29 H4
Park Cl BRKMPK AL9..........29 H5
BRKMPK AL9..........42 C4
Parker Av HERT/WAS SG14..........13 G5
Parkfields WGCE AL8..........19 E2
Parkhurst Rd HERT/WAS SG14..........23 E1
Park La STALE/WH AL4..........40 B1
Park Meadow BRKMPK AL9..........29 H5
Park Ms BRKMPK * AL9..........29 H5
Park Rd HERT/BAY SG13..........23 H2
WARE SG12..........14 C4
Parkside WLYN AL6..........3 H5
Park St BRKMPK AL9..........29 H5
Park Vw BRKMPK AL9..........29 H4
Parkway WGCW AL8..........18 D4
Parkway Cl WGCW AL8..........18 D2
Parkway Gdns WGCW AL8..........18 D3
Parliament Sq HERT/WAS SG14...23 G2
Parnel Rd WGCE SG12..........15 G3
Parsonage La BRKMPK AL9..........41 G1
Parsonage Rd BRKMPK AL9..........41 G1
The Pastures HAT AL10..........35 G2
WARE SG12..........14 D2
WGCE AL7..........19 H4
Peace Gv WLYN AL6..........4 D3
Pearson Av HERT/WAS SG14..........23 F4
Pearsons Cl HERT/BAY SG13..........23 F4
Peartree Cl WGCE AL7..........19 F2
Peartree Ct WGCE AL7..........19 F3
Peartree La WGCE AL7..........19 F3
Peel Crs HERT/WAS SG14..........13 E4
Peg's La HERT/BAY SG13..........23 G3
Pelham Ct WGCE AL7..........20 B3
Pennyfathers La WLYN AL6..........9 H1
Pentley Pk WGCW AL8..........9 E5
Peplins Cl BRKMPK AL9..........42 B4
Peplins Wy BRKMPK AL9..........42 B3
Pepper Hl WGCE SG12..........25 G3
Perrywood WGCW * AL8..........9 E5
Peters Wood Hl WARE SG12..........25 E1
Picketts WGCE AL7..........19 F4
Pine Crest WLYN AL6..........4 B2
Pine Gv BRKMPK AL9..........43 E3
Pinewood WGCE AL7..........19 F4
Pinnate Pl WGCE AL7..........30 B1
Pippens WGCW AL8..........9 E4
Pitsfield WGCW AL8..........9 E4
Pleasant Mt HERT/BAY SG13..........24 D4

Pleasant Ri BRKMPK AL9..........
Ploughmans End WGCE AL7..........
Polayn Garth WGCW AL8..........
Poles La WARE SG12..........
WARE SG12..........
Poles Pk WARE * SG12..........
Pond Ct WLYN * AL6..........
Pond Cft HAT AL10..........
WGCE AL7..........
Pooleys La BRKMPK AL9..........
Popes Rw WARE SG12..........
Popis Gdns WARE SG12..........
Poplar Av HAT AL10..........
Poplar Cl STDN SG11..........
Poplars WGCE AL7..........
Poplars Cl HAT AL10..........
Poppyfields WGCE AL7..........
Port Hl HERT/WAS SG14..........
Portland Pl HERT/BAY SG13..........
Port V HERT/WAS SG14..........
Postfield WGCE AL7..........
Post Office Wk
HERT/WAS * SG14..........
Postwood Gn HERT/BAY SG13..........
Post Wood Rd WARE SG12..........
Potterells BRKMPK * AL9..........
Pottersheath Rd WLYN AL6..........
Poundwell WGCE AL7..........
Poynders Meadow WLYN AL6..........
Presdales Dr WARE SG12..........
Primrose Cl HAT AL10..........
Primrose Dr HERT/BAY SG13..........
Princes St WARE SG12..........
Priors Cl HERT/BAY SG13..........
Priors Wood Rd HERT/BAY SG13...
Priory St HERT/WAS SG14..........
WARE SG12..........
Prospect Pl WLYN AL6..........
Purcell Cl WLYN AL6..........
Purkiss Rd HERT/BAY SG13..........
Puttocks Cl BRKMPK AL9..........
Puttocks Dr BRKMPK AL9..........

Q

The Quadrangle WGCW AL8..........
Quaker Rd WARE SG12..........
Queen's Rd HERT/BAY SG13..........
WARE SG12..........
Queensway HAT AL10..........
Quickbeams WGCE AL7..........
Quincey Rd WARE SG12..........

R

Rabley Heath Rd WLYN AL6..........
Railway Pl HERT/BAY SG13..........
Railway St HERT/WAS SG14..........
Ramblers Wy WGCE AL7..........
Ramsey Cl BRKMPK AL9..........
Raven Ct HAT AL10..........
Rayfield WGCW AL8..........
Raymonds Cl WGCE * AL7..........
Raymonds Pln WGCE AL7..........
Raynham St HERT/BAY SG13..........
Raynsford Rd WARE SG12..........
Rectory Cl BRKMPK AL9..........
Rectory Gdns HAT AL10..........
Rectory Rd WGCW AL8..........
Redan Rd WARE SG12..........
Reddings WGCW AL8..........
Redhall Cl HAT AL10..........
Redhall Dr HAT AL10..........
Red House Cl WARE SG12..........
Redwoods HERT/WAS SG14..........
WGCW AL8..........
The Reeds WGCE AL7..........
Regent Cl WGCE AL7..........
Rendlesham Cl WARE SG12..........
Revels Cl HERT/WAS SG14..........
Revels Rd HERT/WAS SG14..........
Reynards Rd WLYN AL6..........
Reynard Wy HERT/BAY SG13..........
Rib V HERT/WAS SG14..........
Richardson Pl STALE/WH AL4..........
Richmond Cl WARE SG12..........
Rickfield Cl HAT AL10..........
The Riddy WLYN AL6..........
Ridgeway WGCE AL7..........
The Ridgeway HERT/WAS SG14...
WARE SG12..........
WLYN AL6..........
The Ridings HERT/WAS SG14..........
Rivenhall End WGCE AL7..........

WGCE AL7.....19 H1
Westfield Rd HERT/WAS SG14 ...13 F5
Westland Dr BRKMPK AL9 ....42 B5
Westly Wd WGCE AL7.....19 H1
West Md WGCE AL7.....20 A5
Westmill Rd WARE SG12 ....6 A5
West Riding WLYN AL6 ....5 G5
West St HERT/BAY SG13 .....23 F3
  WARE SG12.....15 E4
West Vw HAT AL10.....29 F4
Wheatbarn WGCE AL7....20 A1
Wheatcotes KNEB SG3 .....5 F1
Wheatfield HAT AL10.....29 G5
Wheatley Cl WGCE AL7.....19 H4
Wheatley Rd WGCE AL7 .....19 G3
Wheatsheaf Dr WARE SG12 ....14 C2
Whetstone Cl WLYN AL6.....4 B2
Whitebeams HAT AL10 .....35 F4
White Hl WLYN AL6.....8 B3
White Horse La KNEB SG3 .....5 L1
White Lion Sq HAT AL10 .....29 F5
Whitethorn WGCE AL7.....19 H3
Wicken Flds WARE SG12 ....14 D2
Wickhams Whf WARE * SG12 ...15 F4
The Wick HERT/WAS SG14 ....13 E4

Widbury Gdns WARE SG12 .....15 G4
Widbury Hl WARE SG12.....15 H4
Widford Rd WGCE AL7 ....20 A2
Wigmores North WGCW AL8 ....19 E1
Wildhill Rd BRKMPK AL9 ....36 C4
Wilga Rd WLYN AL6 ....3 G5
Wilkin's Green La
  STALE/WH AL4 .....34 B3
Wilkins Green Ter
  STALE/WH * AL4 ....34 A3
Wilkins Gv WGCW AL8.....19 E3
Willow Gv WGCW AL8 .....9 E2
Willowmead HERT/WAS SG14 ....22 D3
The Willows WARE * SG12.....26 A4
Willow Vw WARE * SG12 .....15 F5
Willow Wk WARE SG12.....3 H2
Willow Wy HAT AL10.....35 E4
Wilshere Rd WLYN AL6.....3 F5
Wilton Crs HERT/BAY SG13.....23 F5
Wilton Rd HERT/BAY SG13 .....23 F4
Winch Cl WLYN * AL6.....3 E2
Windhill WGCE AL7.....19 H1
Winding Shott HERT/WAS SG14...11 H1
Windmill Fld WARE SG12.....15 E5
Windsor Cl WLYN AL6.....8 C2

Windsor Dr HERT/WAS SG14 .....22 C1
Windsor Rd WLYN AL6.....8 C2
Wingate Gdns WLYN * AL6 .....3 C5
Winton Rd WARE SG12.....15 G4
Wistlea Crs STALE/WH AL4 .....34 A5
Witchford WGCE AL7.....20 C2
Woodacre Dr WLYN AL6.....4 D2
Wood Cl HAT AL10.....35 G1
Wood Common HAT AL10.....29 G3
Woodcroft Av WARE SG12 ....26 C4
Woodfield La BRKMPK AL9 .....43 H1
Woodfield Rd WGCE AL7 .....19 G2
Woodhall Cl HERT/WAS SG14 .....13 F5
Woodhall Ct WGCE AL7.....19 F3
Woodhall La WGCE AL7.....19 F4
Woodham Wy WARE SG12 ....26 B4
Woodland Mt HERT/BAY SG13 ....24 A2
Woodland Ri WGCW AL8.....8 D5
Woodland Rd HERT/BAY SG13.....24 D5
Woodlands BRKMPK AL9 ....43 E5
Woodlands Rd HERT/BAY SG13 ...24 A2
  WARE SG12.....7 E4
Woodland Wy WGCW AL6 .....4 C3
Woodley Rd WARE SG12.....15 G3
Woodpecker Cl HAT * AL10 ....35 E4

Woods Av HAT AL10.....35 F2
Woodside HERT/BAY SG13 ....24 D5
Woodside La BRKMPK AL9 ....36 C4
Woodside Rd WLYN AL6 .....9 G2
Woodstock Cl HERT/BAY SG13...24 C4
Wood V HAT AL10.....35 G1
Woolmers La HERT/WAS SG14 ....32 C1
Worcester Rd HAT AL10.....29 F5
Wordsworth Ct HAT * AL10 .....29 F5
Wren Wd WGCE AL7.....20 A1
Wulfrath Wy WARE SG12 .....14 D2
Wyddial Gn WGCE AL7.....20 C2
Wyndhams End BRKMPK AL9 ....30 C1
Wyton WGCE AL7.....20 C2

Y

Yearling Cl WARE SG12 .....25 G2
Yew Gv WGCE AL7.....20 B3
York Wy WLYN AL6.....8 C2
Youngsbury La WARE SG12 .....7 E1
Youngs Ri WGCW AL8.....18 C

Index - featured places

Activity World
  HAT AL10.....29 G3
All Nations Christian College
  WARE SG12.....26 A1
Alpha Business Park
  BRKMPK AL9.....41 H1
Amwell View School (Special)
  WARE SG12.....26 A4
Applecroft JMI School
  WGCW AL8.....18 C2
Barn Theatre
  WGCW AL8.....18 D2
Bayford Primary School
  HERT/BAY SG13.....39 G1
Bengeo J & I School
  HERT/WAS SG14.....13 F4
Bircherley Green
  Shopping Centre
  HERT/WAS SG14.....23 G2
Birchwood Leisure Centre
  HAT AL10.....29 G3
Birchwood Primary School
  HAT AL10.....29 F4
Bishops Hatfield Girls School
  HAT AL10.....35 F1
Bishops Square Business Park
  HAT AL10.....28 D5
  HAT AL10.....35 F5
Blackthorn Junior School
  WGCE AL7.....19 H3
Bridgegate Business Centre
  WGCE AL7.....19 G1
Briggens House Hotel Golf Club
  WARE SG12.....27 H5
Brookmans Park Golf Club
  BRKMPK AL9.....42 D3
Brookmans Park
  Primary School
  BRKMPK AL9.....42 B4
Campus West Cinema
  WGCW AL8.....19 E1
Campus West Leisure Centre
  WGCW AL8.....18 D1
Castle Hall Theatre &
  Civic Centre
  HERT/WAS SG14.....23 F2
Chadwell Springs Golf Club
  WARE SG12.....14 D5
Chancellors School
  BRKMPK AL9.....43 E3
The Chauncy School
  WARE SG12.....14 C3
Christ Church Primary School
  WARE SG12.....15 F4
Church Street Industrial Estate
  WARE SG12.....15 E3
Codicote JMI School
  WLYN AL6.....2 D1
The Collingwood Suite
  Conference Centre
  WGCW AL8.....18 D4
Colney Heath JMI School
  STALE/WH AL4.....34 B5
Commonswood JMI School
  WGCE AL7.....20 A5

Corn Exchange
  HERT/WAS SG14.....23 G2
Countess Anne Primary School
  HAT AL10.....29 G5
Creswick Primary School
  WGCE AL7.....19 E5
Duncombe School
  HERT/WAS SG14.....23 F1
Epping House School
  HERT/BAY SG13.....38 D4
Ermine Point Business Park
  WARE SG12.....14 C1
Essendon Primary School
  BRKMPK AL9.....32 A5
Fiddlebridge Industrial Centre
  HAT AL10.....29 F5
Five Oaks Primary School
  HAT AL10.....35 F3
Forum Theatre
  HAT AL10.....29 E5
Frobisher Way Hatfield
  Business Park
  HAT AL10.....29 E4
Galleria Shopping Centre
  HAT AL10.....35 E1
The Garden City Practice
  WGCE AL7.....19 E1
Garden Court Business Centre
  WGCE AL7.....19 G2
Gosling Ski & Board Centre
  WGCW AL8.....18 D4
Gosling Sports Park
  WGCW AL8.....18 D4
Green Lanes Primary School
  WGCE AL7.....29 E2
Haslemere Industrial Estate
  WGCE AL7.....19 G1
Hatfield Business Park
  HAT AL10.....28 C3
  HAT AL10.....34 D1
Hatfield House
  BRKMPK AL9.....36 A1
Hatfield Leisure Centre
  HAT AL10.....35 G3
Hatfield London Country Club
  BRKMPK AL9.....38 A2
Hatfield Swim Centre
  HAT AL10.....29 F5
Hazelgrove Primary School
  HAT AL10.....35 E4
Hertford County Hospital
  HERT/WAS SG14.....23 E2
Hertford Museum
  HERT/WAS SG14.....23 G2
Hertford Regional College
  WARE SG12.....15 E5
Hertford St Andrew
  Primary School
  HERT/WAS SG14.....22 C1
Hertfordshire Country Club
  WGCE AL7.....19 E5
Hertford Town FC
  HERT/WAS SG14.....23 E3
Hollybush Primary School
  HERT/WAS SG14.....22 D2

Holwell J & I School
  WGCE AL7.....19 G3
Home Farm Industrial Estate
  WARE SG12.....27 E3
Homerswood J & I School
  WGCW AL8.....9 E3
The Howard Centre
  WGCE AL7.....19 E2
Howe Dell Primary School
  HAT AL10.....35 G1
Kingshill Primary School
  WARE SG12.....15 E2
Knightsfield School
  WGCW AL8.....8 D2
Lakeside Special School
  WGCW AL8.....18 C4
The Maltings Industrial Estate
  WARE SG12.....26 C4
Marriott Hanbury Manor Golf &
  Country Club
  WARE SG12.....6 D5
Marshgate Trading Estate
  HERT/BAY SG13.....23 H1
Martinfield Business Centre
  WGCE AL7.....19 G1
The Mead Business Centre
  HERT/BAY SG13.....23 H1
Mercers College
  WARE SG12.....15 E3
Middleton Special School
  WARE SG12.....25 E1
Mill Green Golf Club
  BRKMPK AL9.....30 C2
Mill Mead J & I School
  HERT/WAS SG14.....23 F2
Mill Studio Business Centre
  WARE SG12.....15 F4
Monks Walk School
  WGCW AL8.....8 D2
Morgans JMI School
  HERT/BAY SG13.....23 G4
Morgans Junior School
  HERT/BAY SG13.....23 G4
Morgans Walk Junior
  Mixed School
  HERT/WAS SG14.....22 D4
Musley Infant School
  WARE SG12.....15 F3
New Briars Primary School
  HAT AL10.....35 F1
North Mymms Cricket Club
  BRKMPK AL9.....41 H4
Oaklands College
  HAT AL10.....35 F1
  WGCW AL8.....19 E1
Oaklands JMI School
  WLYN AL6.....4 B3
Onslow St Audreys School
  HAT AL10.....35 G1
Our Ladys RC Primary School
  WGCE AL7.....19 F4
Panshanger Aerodrome
  WGCE AL7.....20 D2
Panshanger Golf &
  Squash Complex
  WGCE AL7.....10 B5

Panshanger JMI School
  WGCE AL7.....19 H
The Pines Primary School
  HERT/BAY SG13.....24 E
Pinewood Special School
  WARE SG12.....25 E
Ponsbourne Tunnel
  HERT/BAY SG13.....39 H
Potterells Medical Centre
  BRKMPK AL9.....42 A
Presdales School
  WARE SG12.....15
Priors Wood JMI School
  WARE SG12.....15
Queen Elizabeth II Hospital
  BRKMPK AL9.....30
Queensway Health Centre
  HAT AL10.....29
Queen Victoria
  Memorial Hospital
  WLYN AL6.....8
Real Tennis Club
  BRKMPK AL9.....36
Richard Hale School
  HERT/BAY SG13.....23
Rowans Primary School
  WGCE AL7.....9
The Ryde Primary School
  BRKMPK AL9.....30
Sacred Heart RC
  Primary School
  WARE SG12.....14
St Andrews Primary School
  WARE SG12.....26
St Johns CE J & I (Mixed) School
  WGCW AL8.....18
St Johns CE Primary School
  WLYN AL6.....9
St John the Baptist
  Primary School
  WARE SG12.....25
St Marys Junior School
  WARE SG12.....15
St Marys Primary School
  BRKMPK AL9.....41
  WLYN AL6.....8
St Philip Howard Catholic
  Primary School
  HAT AL10.....35
Salisbury Infant School
  HAT AL10.....35
School of Art & Design
  HAT AL10.....29
Scott's Grotto
  WARE SG12.....15
The Sele School
  HERT/WAS SG14.....2
Sherrardswood School
  WLYN AL6.....
Simon Balle School
  HERT/BAY SG13.....2
Sir Frederic Osborn School
  WGCE AL7.....2
Sir John Newsom School
  WGCE AL7.....1